On GLASSY WINGS

On GLASSY WINGS

POEMS NEW & SELECTED

Anne SZUMIGALSKI

COTEAU BOOKS

Edited by Don Kerr.

Cover and book design by Duncan Campbell.
Printed and bound in Canada.

The publisher gratefully acknowledges the financial assistance of the
Saskatchewan Arts Board, the Canada Council for the Arts,
the Department of Canadian Heritage, and the City of Regina
Arts Commission, for its publishing programme.

Canadian Cataloguing in Publication Data

Szumigalski, Anne, 1922-
On glassy wings
ISBN 1-55050-114-3

1. Title.
PS8587.Z44O54 1997   C811'.54   C97-920098-9
PR9199.3.S985O54 1997

COTEAU BOOKS
401-2206 Dewdney Avenue
Regina, Saskatchewan
S4R 1H3

AVAILABLE IN THE U.S. FROM:
General Distribution Services
85 River Rock Road, suite 202
Buffalo, New York, USA, 14207

For my brother John Allen Davis
And in memory of his wife Madeleine

Eternity is in love
with the productions of time.
—WILLIAM BLAKE
FROM *A Memorable Fancy*

It is the essence of poetry
that always it does not yet exist.
But it will.
—MIROSLAV HOLUB
FROM *Sagittal Section*

FOREWORD i

Theirs Is The Song *1*

OUR SULLEN ART

Our Sullen Art *7*
Skeps in the Orchard *8*
Fennec *10*
Her Mother Being Dead in One Way or Another *11*
Want of Þ Want of Ð *12*
His Method *14*
Videotape *15*
The Musicologist *19*
Hedera Helix—The Spiral *21*
The Dove *22*
The Bear *24*
Flick 1938 *26*
I Put On My Gloves *28*
FROM *Risks* *30*
Evangelium *33*
Crabseeds *34*
A House With A Tower *35*

YOUR CHILD LOOKS UP

Classification *39*
Where Are You Arthur Silverman? *40*
Third Trimester *42*
The Cranes *43*

Halinka 44

Mater Dolorosa 45

Your Child Looks Up 46

The Boy at the Upstairs Window With His Head in His Hands 47

The Cloud 48

The Varying Hare 50

Honny 52

Ferret 55

Heroines 58

Grey-eyed Frances 62

Daisy Filman 63

Lavinia 65

Ribgrass 67

Nettles 68

Childermas Three 69

Desire

As So Many Do 73

Desire 74

Under the Glare of the Sun 75

It Wasn't a Major Operation 77

Ergot and After 78

On Parting 80

On Loneliness 81

On Singleness 83

Long Distance 85

Bertha 86

Annwfn 87

Hanner Hwch Hanner Hob—The Flitch 89

Mates 91

In Praise of My Own Breasts 93

Victim 94
Aunt's Story 95
Early Sorrow 97
Stopover 99
A Game of Angels 101
Prospect House 102
In the Wilderness 103

ABOUT MY WAR

Looking for Uncle Tich in the War Cemetery 107
Making up a Four 108
An Offering 109
Patrick Valentine 111
Shrapnel 112
The Name of Our City 114
What A Girl Has 116
Sitting Under Death's Rich Shade 117
Burning The Stubble 119
About My War 120
The Arrangement 122
Summer 1928 124

SHE IMPORTUNES GOD

Woman Reading in Bath 129
Alice Long 131
Viaticum—The Text 132
Gerald 135
The Compassion 137
The Holy Fountain 138

The Man from Toledo   *139*
Granny Looks at the Stars   *141*
Wise Queenie, Wise Queen   *144*
Passover   *145*
Green   *146*
A Girl Dreams   *148*

DEATH AND OTHER ABSTRACTIONS

Between One Thing and Another   *153*
Bigos   *154*
The Restoration   *155*
The Farm   *156*
In The Heat Of The Morning   *158*
Paradijslaan   *159*
On Grieving   *161*
The Usual Dream About One's Funeral   *163*
$i^2 = -1$ *165*
The Disc   *166*
The Margin   *167*
A Celebration   *168*

A THISTLE CALLED HOLY

On the Sun   *173*
Purple   *175*
The Bees   *177*
Dusk   *179*
The Undoing   *180*
Siôn Forest   *182*
Flatbread   *184*

Naked on the Shore   185
Our First Gods Were Fishes   187
The Elephant Dream   189
The Burning Man   190
The Elect   192
What is a Man To Do   193
The Fall   194
Malus   196
A Thistle Called Holy   197
Industrial Park—Midsummer   198

On The Nature And History Of Angels   203

AFTERWORD 209

SOURCE INDEX 215

SOME NOTES ON THE POEMS 219

ABOUT THE AUTHOR 221

FOREWORD

I've always been amazed by the poetry of Anne Szumigalski, not only because it's so good, but because I can never predict "what in the world is coming next," to quote Grace Paley. Her imagination has nothing in common with my own. She's like another country, even if she does live in Saskatoon on Connaught Place and we've been reading prose and poetry at each other for a dozen years now in one of her writing groups. Familiarity continues to breed surprise. I've read interviews in which Anne talks about her poetry, but that doesn't help. The surprises continue, as they do with the wonderful new poems in this book.

Anne and I have been co-editors on and off since 1973 when we were associate editors on *Grain* under Caroline Heath. Anne and I even got poems into *Grain* over Caroline's objection, at least twice in eight years, maybe three times. We edited *Heading Out* in 1986, an anthology of new Saskatchewan poets, and an issue of *Grain* in 1990 on writing in Saskatoon. Both are cross-sections of the Saskatchewan writing community. I edited Anne's last book, *Voice,* for Coteau. I was able to help with the prose, but my major suggestion on the poems was to remove two lines—then we thought better of that radical move.

Here's how we worked on the "selected" part of the *Poems New & Selected*. Anne and I each made our choices book by book in chronological order. We'd meet over one book, then the next, and so on. Anne had her choices, I had mine. Sometimes they were the same, as often they were not, which was a new editing experience, since we'd had a high level of agreement in all our earlier ventures. We'd talk about the poems; a few would disappear from the list. When we'd completed our selection we had to find categories for them, since Anne wanted a thematic not a chronological arrangement. There were always some obvious categories: poems on war, poems on God, poems on art, and slowly we found the others—the one on earth and water, which we called "A Thistle Called Holy," is I think especially useful in focusing on one of Anne's lifelong interests.

Of course the categories are very leaky. For example, "The Bear" is a poem on war, on an animal, and on art, where we placed it. "Purple" is on the purple loosestrife, and on God. The last sentence of "The Compassion" points two ways: "yet by/faith we see buds as the angels who are god's pupils/see us." The conclusion to "Bigos" is a good way to look at Anne's world and the perviousness of categories:

> All night the lovers scrape and scour. Will they
> never be able to divide one substance from another?

Of course there are omissions. One are the prose pieces that have become a feature of Anne's last two books—and "Ferret" is the closest to those works here. It was easy to choose some of Anne's obviously good pieces like "Theirs is the Song," "Her Mother Being Dead," "Summer 1928," and so on, but very difficult to draw the line at the other end. We had agreed with Coteau that a book of about 200 pages sounded right, so that was the limit we worked within, and have omitted over half of Anne's poems. The best way to read a poet is entire, as I've had the pleasure of doing. But *On Glassy Wings: Poems New & Selected* has its special interest too, since the poems are organized in groups chosen by Anne that may help people to read her in a new way.

Most of Anne's poems I already knew, but I had never read *Journey/Journée*, her book with Terrence Heath, and in reading it, with great pleasure, I returned to those writing years in Saskatoon, and somewhere in the middle of that book I asked myself which is more real, Anne, who I will meet again in a week, or these poems which I'm now meeting for the first time? That strange thought hasn't left. Are we most ourselves or the second skins we slough off as poems?

Enjoy the Anne Szumigalski you meet in this book. She travels very well.

—Don Kerr

3.25

i

Seabirds stopped in their flight
are perched on clouds
as on hedges of mist.

Worms lift blunt muzzles
from their beds of sludge;
since the birds are silent
theirs is the song,
rasping as it comes from their mouths'
ten thousand straightt pink slits.

A woman walking on the seafront
ties a flimsy scarf round her head
the silk so thin
her wind-burned ears poke through.

She looks up and sees men jump
from their dark moving palace in the sky,
descending like delicate mushrooms
with double stipes.

The sun burns the lips of the waves
until they crisp and fold over,
pancakes ready for jam and cream,
for foam and red tides.

Dead fish have stained the sea
with their amber tears.
Their skeletons are harps of sharp white bones
silent in the mud.

Bubbles prickle the water.
The woman bends. She reads

history from ancient texts scribbled
on the shells swept in by the tide,

stories of dolphin and urchin
coral and shark
smudged by her thumbs.

ii

The reason for the sky is the Earth,
for the Earth the sky.

Somewhere beyond the ether
angels are battling out
that ancient war between colours,
black and white,
silver and gold
their wings.

Their eyes green and grey.
Their open mouths showing red tunnels of song.

Here on Earth we have other things to fight about:
how many shillings in a bag,
how many chimneys make a stack.

Will there ever be a day when we understand
numbers, where they start
and how they flourish and fade?

As for the angels, they have singed their feathers
in the heat of this question:
when exactly does yellow become orange,
where do these two divide?

While in Heaven God struggles with equations,
trying to balance the universe.

iii

How dear to her is the journey of the mind,
flying from dwelling to dwelling,

Her feet scraping the tops of the
forest trees as she floats on by,

Exchanging one language for another,
never quite sure of her bearings,
counting the chimneys on unfamiliar roofs.

One day she hopes to understand progression
how it has no end and no beginning,
how nothing precedes or succeeds,
how time is a disc that wobbles
as it spins.

The melody is an old one
played again and again.
All night she's aware that it scuttles
over the pillows like a louse on holiday.

Waking she hears it emerge from her nose,
a hum like paperwasps.

"But that's just the tune," she says,
"tomorrow on my way I'll write the words."

Our
SULLEN
ART

the language of poetry has something to do
with the open mouth the tongue that jumps
up and down like a child on a shed roof calling
ha ha and who's the dirty rascal now?
the same boy sent to his room for punishment
leans from his window listening for animals
far away in the woods strains his ears to catch
even the slightest sound of rage but nothing howls
even the hoot of owls in the dusk is gentle

he hears the tiny snarl of the shrew
the rasp of the snail's foot on the leaf
the too-high squeaking of bats which comes
to his head as the vibration
of distant hacksaws   he hum humms
with his lips tight shut he stands there
listening and humming almost through the short night
then   falls into the tangle of sheets and blankets
where fitfully he sleeps while slowly
the window greys to four panes of bleak light

the day's first traffic travels carefully
past the windows and doors of the shut house
so as not to awaken in the child
those savage cries our violent
our pathetic language of poems

Skeps In The Orchard

we signed the contract

your part was to lie in the orchard
every afternoon and sleep
mine was to sit and watch you
until you wakened

when autumn came
it was rather chilly for both of us
I folded my shoulders into a blanket
as you slept
your breath rose whitely
into the cool air

the shape of your breath is a cone
it is the shape of inside silence
called null
and from the cone's tip
a word is squeezed out
the word is
worm
worm
worm

the word is latent
the word is fishhook

the word has no sound
it has only a shape
O O O
tip of a needle
is a steel cone
it could get broken
into your finger sewing

it could travel up your arm
and about and around you
until it felt your heart's pull
and pierced itself in

your head is a fat cone
wound with heavy brown hair

or

with soft white hair

or

all the hair could fall out
and show your round head
dull newborn mouse pink
and then a word could be written on your head
with the gray cone tip of a lead pencil

the word is grist
        thistle
        brush
        cerise

words are hive bees
each has the shape of its hum
a winged O

they are flying home in a formation
with the shape of a curved blade
returning to the straw hive
with its knotted tip

my nibs and quills arranged before me on a stained deal table I am designing the alphabet for a new language called in that tongue *speech of the foxes* because the consonants fall on the ear like the yipping of reynard in the henrun   because when a woman enunciates the vowels they sound the human cry of a vixen in heat

precisely I fill in the empty eyes of the letters with slit-shaped green ink *viridian* it says on the bottle *lamp black* on the tube I pick for the pupils

with a blade I scrape flaky rust from the window-catch then spit and mix a reddish pigment brush between the letters cursive loops that crouch and slink across the page

I'm weary with invention cannot find the strength to reject an idea for punctuation: two small triangles a pair of pricked-up ears

Her Mother Being Dead In One Way Or Another

1. since you read that novel about a bald woman her tribulations her wigs and disguises you can always discover in yourself a small space where she lies curled in effigy aching in her hairlessness

2. then you picked up a book about napoleon how he was the ultimate victim of arsenic   how tedious it is that this idea keeps coming back every ten years with slight variations in the evidence—the analysis of a single hair the discovery of a secret code locked in a journal

3. then there are fictions of men watching women brush back their hair from brows delicate as a rabbit's   the men declare their excitement when all along their true desire is to be female themselves, to experience silk rubbing against silk between empty thighs

4. you close your book and imagine yourself walking alone at night in a white shift ignoring the presence of a young man who leans from the upstairs window of the next house   he watches you flit on bare feet down a path illumined only by a moon no bigger than a coin

5. the youth is composing a poem about a woman walking alone in a garden at night   his words take everything into account excepting only the sudden transformation of a forthright child into a young girl who longs to give herself entirely to the pleasure of another's will   is there no one to defend her from herself

6. his words deaf to this question are busy arranging themselves on a tornout flyleaf   they speak of the tattered clouds that stain the sky   they speak of a dark trickle that becomes a river eventually throwing itself from a stony cliff into the sea

7. the young man takes his time thinking up titles for this piece one is *the emergency* another is *chalkline* a third is *the trend*

stitch in the side
thorn in the mouth
between tongue and teeth
carmen the glowing carmine of the rose

what happens
going home after the dance?
it's thrown aside
droops its red head
on the gravel of the road
that leads away from the factory

the flower signifies a man at arms
his ceremonial strut
or could be a guerilla lying
at ambush in the long ditch grass

these fall, both cast in the sand
of someone else's glory
while each word held above
the shifting air thins
to less than a syllable

an unvoiced thorn
anther anthem
the easter church
swirls with spring pollen
two young sisters lift their arms
their hands deck the windowsills
with primrose and sallow
catkin exhaling that heady
stink of sap   a veil
for each newly-confirmed head
here follows in quires the anthem
rising like smoke
from their virginal fires

mother has clothed them in neat frocks
with wide quaker collars
before summer brings the rose
whose red dye stains the lips
its thorns like cigarettes

what have we left to us
at our age? one sister writes
you wanted to judge
I wanted to pronounce
sentences   neither of us
kept to our maiden calling

(ah the red-stained tongue
between nicotine teeth)

edh edh something always missing
from the mouth   laziness
at the foundry
loss at the font
a blank in the vocabulary
of desire *loth love that tethers thee*
it's a gap grin

and so we lisp on to the grave
sons and daughters follow
the book on the lectern closes
the purple cloth pulled over
the ancient face now fades
the primrose, withers the rose
what was it that we suffered
that we shared?
lack of a letter for an apidental sound?

this sharp and sudden pain in the side
the compositor's error

his method was to bully the poem his habit to address it in the second person singular as though it was a servant or a deity   he would not let the piece end for he simply could not trust it to come to a worthwhile conclusion unfinished as it was he would pin it to a branch of his serviceberry to dry the ink to give the thing a bit of fresh air a bit of an outside view   then he'd go upstairs and watch it from his bedroom window as it fluttered about trying to break the grip of the clothespin urging itself to take off in the wind   *thou fool* he shouted *thou fool*   but the window was double-glazed and the sash was painted shut so that no sound issued into the open air   the words jumped back into his mouth and he was forced to swallow them   there he stood all afternoon and when the sun set he saw it as wildfire attacking the paper the clothespin the branch in the end the whole tree was blazing   *the dialogue is over* he conceded for after all neither man nor god can play his part without a script

somewhere in Russia
Kakky is dancing
Kakky is dancing in a shiny shift
Kakky is dancing on her bare flat feet
        shaking her belly
        shaking her shirt
        shaking her hair out till it
        breaks and falls
        on her square feet dusty from the floor

a hundred are watching
moving their slow eyes
side to side with her undulations where
   the breasts show in the cleft   where the yellow silk parted
                and where the lips   part
tombstone teeth glimmering between redbrown lips

     all they say is AH   all they do is wonder what the mad life is
            hung somewhere between Greece and Africa
                somewhere between movement and desire
what the drum is
what the dream is   don't tell me this is WESTERN
                                DECADENCE
        Mr. Lecturer
        Mr. Lecher how could he look?
                how could he find time
                to time the beat of her feet
on the splinters?
        stare eyes at the dust from the floorboards
virtues greet all the jerks with horror
what's a life without purpose?
                        purpose me only to roll about
                            in a bed of love

Saint Katharine come down
                come down from the
shaking film Saint Katharine
miraculously moving ikon   girl of the gods   devotee of life
                newly nubile   dance
                                dance round Russia
Kakky till blisters numb your feet

                reel over till
            the reel over breathing vodka
        we   all reel out to the gray street
        high over Russia
        the wide heavy aircraft slowly roars
        full of heavy Soviet Peoples above
                and below the clouds
                on the plain
                on the steppe
                highgrass and lowgrass
                ridge and cold mountain
        they are standing everywhere
        staring up at salvation crying

send us only life and breath and fire and Kakky wound in a tin box

throw it down
on our tower
in our town let us gather in a hut of corrugated sheets
                    gather and wonder
                    worship and revile

O miraculous ribbon unravel the mystery
O let us sit solid
        and stolid   and watch Kakky dancing
            three times through

caught like a reed
    in the squeeze
    and the freeze of the North night
          where the North Light   is all that is green until
May   and how many
days until then?
    when something might
          spring in
          spring beside the flood from the
        slipping glaciers every day measuring icebergs as they
fall and slowly turn in a dignified dance in the sea
all the long night is illumined
with candles of devotion all the
snow in the boring streets can't
smother the sound of footsteps
in the dark running to the Peop
les' Palace room 42 where a small
man in a brown jacket will proje
      ct for the eighth time the strong stamp and beat
                  of Kakky's fat feet
        and the sudden and certain jerk of her spine

but the picture fades and film flickers and is broken
the sound whistles
  and wavers and dies
          celluloid stretched and
            shredded to ribbons
boxes with rusted rims
dumped in the
dump
      after a year or two years or
        ten years who will remember
      Kakky's buckteeth?
      or the kink of her coarse dark hair?

as the crystal bears the cutting beam
Kakky is dancing in Russia
for there are girls
  glad to be
       wet
       warm and
       willing   they are dancing out of all the houses
and bringing down planes from the skies
    demanding devotion with the strong beat of their hot bare
                                       feet and the slap
of their breasts
on their chests
and the sting of the sweat that runs into their eyes

lately her friend d has moved into the city to study the sounds of extinct tramways and long-abandoned circus stops   everywhere he goes he carries a tape recorder and an old yellow copybook the cover inked all over with gracenotes in black marker

he plays her a tape of bales of cotton being thrown down from the upper windows of an old brickfaced warehouse   when she presses the machine to her ear she can just make out the whoosh and thud of the bales as they fall into the moored barge and the faint voices of the wharfers *loohoutbelow loohoutbelow*   d shows her the place in the notebook where he's written down the melody all the sounds that ever were are stored in the void around us he claims   the basis of some sort of symphony she asks   he snorts with laughter at her simplistic approach

in an empty lot where once the rag-and-bone man's donkey grazed at noon after a meagre nosebag she stands in the weeds while d is busy getting the old codger to belt out his cry at the proper distance from the mike *ragaboooooone ragaboooooone raga-boooooone* and so on then out comes the notebook this time for the donkey which gives a bray more like a scream when it cuts its lip on a rusted tin can lying in the grass

twopence for a jamjar
threepence for an old straw hat
for mo to wear at his wedding-o
croons the old man hugging the donkey's head wiping the wound with a wodge of fresh grass the poor creature gives a long sigh of pain and affection   for a moment she thinks she sees tears of pity in d's eyes then she realizes it is only one of his professional ecstasies everything is music to the trained ear he says and hums a bar or two from this and that century

on saturday she goes to the luncheonette where d works weekends playing the marimba for six bucks an hour faster faster demands the manager and who can blame him for everyone knows that the faster the music the faster people eat so d plays on and on with dishes rattling and cigarette smoke rising all around his sweaty forehead on and on faster and faster while she imagines that when he stops the eating and yelling and crashing of crockery will cease then the customers and the animals that have followed them into this place will get up on their hind legs and applaud him with a long moment of silence you spend your time fashioning blue glass eyes from which grow fronds of porcelain flowers delicately laquered   once in a while the flowers remind you of crabapple blossoms when this happens you have to concentrate very hard not to let the twig grow into a branch, the branch grow into a tree whose gnarled roots could obscure the clear blue iris

years ago you were employed in a toy factory making bisque heads for dolls   as you lifted each head from the sagger you held it to the light and pencilled in the surprised dark eyebrows then you dipped into red and coloured the nostrils and parted lips

one day you noticed that your left hand had taken up a pinch of white clay and was modelling a trail of ivy issuing like a word from the doll's mouth   now it is eyes always eyes, their budding glances, their flowering tears

THE DOVE

It troubles the boy that, if you want to draw a white bird, you must use a black pencil—or, at least a dark grey one. A drawing can never get away from its hard outline.

His aunt promises him that tomorrow she will buy him black paper and white chalk, and he can try again.

"No," says the boy obstinately, "for when the sky is black it is night, and no one can see anything, not even a white bird. You can hear the whirr of her wings as she passes. That is all."

"Perhaps," suggests his aunt, "it could be moonlight."

It's bedtime, and the woman places the drawing on the nightstand beside her nephew. Then she kisses him and leaves, shutting the door softly, but decisively, behind her.

The boy puts his hands over his eyes and pretends to sleep. Through his fingers he can just make out the drawing peeling itself from the page and flying away into the dark. The bird has abandoned him to his dreams.

During the long night, the child comes to the understanding that the bird is in some way his mother.

The drawing itself, he knows, is his own creature and must obey him. The bird, on the other hand, is free to follow all her whims and desires.

It is morning, and he wakes to the closed-in light of snowfall. Barefoot and tiptoe on the cold roses of the linoleum, he stares through the window. The garden and the road beyond are a single space of trackless white.

On the sill he notices a small curved feather. It could have come from his pillow of course, but maybe his aunt has placed it there, in hopes of comforting him a little for his loss.

Suspicious and grave, he takes up his crayons and gives the bird her colours: glossy yellow wings, an emerald poll, a blue breast speckled with red.

The bird is now more splendid than his mother ever was. Pinned to the paper with the brilliance of her plumage, she will never be able to escape again.

THE BEAR

Flat calm, and you're coming in
To Ostend on paquet or hovercraft

Riding a disturbance of spray
Watching the sun melt
Into the sea. Flowing

In just that same way as tin from the ore
And you're thinking, no conqueror

Has come the other way for a very long time—
Nine hundred years since the Bastard.

All those Saxon heads
Lie buried under the fields
Of Hastings

And those swords put up,
The keen edge rusting away.

They were picked up and smelted again,
Steel to steel, iron to iron,

To plough, to stove
And then to sword again.

Now the same metal serves
As the railings of a park,

And in the park, a zoo,
And a cage, and a bear in the cage
Dusty and irascible.

This is *Ursus americanus*
Hardly distinguishable from *Ursus arctos*

The true European; but this bear comes,
You know, from our own woods

Where once a photographer angered a she-bear
Into posing. *Shutter, shutter, click-click*

He baited her, *it won't hurt a bit darling.*
The bear stood still

And then reached out to him,
Ripped his chest with sickle claws.

Her portrait fell
To the forest floor unharmed

The print showed simply a huge paw,
And the terrified face of a man,
His mouth open on a shriek.

It won first prize in a competition,
Images of Fear and Hate.

The man in the movie is playing his trumpet at breakfast. It shines too brightly for words. He is carried away by the music, by the steam from his mug of coffee.

Isn't that the same tune you played at the Club Casino last night? The young woman dressed in lustrous satin pyjamas is leaning against a post of the arbour. She's been picking dark heart-shaped roses. Her feelings are obvious from the way she slopes her body as she turns her face and her attention to the light which plays on her cheekbones, showing the delicate hollows in the corners of her mouth. Her lips are dewy grey, her teeth are glistening white beads.

Far in the background a tiny girl dances down a flight of steps. Anyone can tell that the child is tapping out the story of her lost innocence.

The woman begins to place the flowers in a black crystal vase but as she turns to smile at the trumpeter she knocks over her careful arrangement. Shining water drowns the breakfast. It falls in a white cascade over the edge of the table.

The man puts down his instrument to help her clear up the mess. He snatches off her scarf to mop at the spill. An obvious faux pas, for this is the scarf her father brought home from a small war somewhere on another continent. A flashback, dimmed by artificial fog, shows him driving a tank towards the ocean gazing at a crumpled snapshot of his tiny daughter. He holds it in a cold hand, in a ragged mitt.

The suave young man picks up his trumpet and plays his heart out, wail, wail, O tremulo but the woman is not to be comforted. How can she forgive a man who is in love with his trumpet? He holds it so passionately, his mouth pressed to its metal.

Imperiously she gestures for him to leave. He does so jauntily, so as not to show his wounded pride. His silent instrument droops under his arm.

And there she stands, quite alone now, forever tilting her face carefully towards the camera.

I put on my gloves and examine a hawthorn leaf. How like it is to my hand, my fingers. Just last spring I spent the best part of a week picking small furry caterpillars from these same shrubs. For some time afterwards I could neither knit nor write for the creatures' hollow hairs turned out to be so many miniature hypodermic needles injecting me with a cloudy yellowish fluid which caused the eruption of itching blisters. Soon the infection had travelled to my head; there it became a sickness of the mind, and I was troubled by dreams of suffocation and meta-morphosis.

On the first day of my convalescence I received a letter from my mother, telling me that in her youth it had been proved beyond a doubt that DDT would eventually alter the eyesight and hear-ing of everyone within a five-mile radius of its application. This set me wondering how it is that I have never been able to write a satisfactory poem about farm chemicals. No matter what time of day I sit down to this task, I at once hear the drone of a small plane overhead and am convinced that it's a cropduster spraying whatever it is they use nowadays to keep down the little chig-gers and wrigglers—and the weeds of course. Behind the hum of the engine I can clearly hear a voice explaining that there are always at least three sides to every question.

Not long after that I was visited by an earnest fellow whose obsession was the fluoridation of public water. *It will all catch up with us in the end,* he insisted, *we'll see our noses grow into snouts and our eyes get smaller and rheumier. We won't even notice that we are trotting about on all fours and rooting in the midden. In fact there's plenty of evidence that swine, those coarse and glori-ous creatures, were once very like us, but that of course was before they fell to tinkering with the environment.*

What a waste of time were those April days when I swung in a grubby string hammock on the porch. Looking out over the greening lawn, I tried to tell myself that words after all are nothing more than beetles in the grass looking for a taller stem to climb so as to see how far they have strayed from home. *Quite far enough,* they conclude, and hasten down again.

L and Crystal notice/that adversity has brought
them closer/that they are becoming used to each
other/that they are becoming each other/this is
disappointing/because their genitals/ which were
so important to them/are of no account any more/

they try to hide them with pieces of paper torn
from L's typewriter/the paper is covered with
disregarded similes/which fall from their pages/
having been absolved/having been let go/to lead
a life of their own/they would much rather be
part of an extended family/a poem as long as
your arm/

the similes have a grievance/they feel they ought
to be allowed to tell the whole story from their
point of view/they arrange a meeting at the expense
of a government agency/L gets wind of it/he arrives
there first/he stands in front of the door with his
arms folded/telling them to fuck off/

L/Crystal is now so tired
that he/she falls to the floor
of his/her little home in the west
he/she is so tired that exhaustion nets up hair
breath voice into a foggy veil, a pall on
their past separation
the shack becomes a house of sleep
whose windows and doors are dreams

next morning L awakens alone
in his room and searches
everywhere for his poem

at last he finds a tiny glass bead
stuck between the floorboards
now he must make up his mind
whether to store it safely
in his penny-candy jar
or to recycle it by swallowing

just for something to do
L sits down at the typewriter
"Understanding" he types "is connected
in a very special way to metaphor
and the use of diverse and diffuse images:

What quickens the work of certain masters
is their continuing use of listed similes.
This brings to mind the familiar
snaking highways and byways of the
tradition-oriented thought-process....."

he tips back his chair
to admire his work
he tells himself
he has written something
which will last

The crystal in the jar begins to cry/it mewls
and rages against him/shrieks in an enraged
glass voice/jumps out of the jar and lodges in
his gullet/it is a dry crust he has swallowed/
it is a hook in the mouth of a fish/

L is forced to recant
he swears off poetics forever

it is the late morning of a dull day
L notices a spit of rain against the window
soon it turns to sleet, and later to snow

he remembers his grandmother telling him
that angels are plucking geese in heaven
when it snows here on earth

watching the down fall from heaven
he thinks he can smell the old farm smell
of ducks and geese hung by their feet
on barndoor nails
their yellow bills dangling
he thinks of ducklice and goose fleas
crawling distractedly between the soft feathers
and the cooling flesh
the fleas and the lice bite and bite
but the blood has congealed
there is no more dinner for them
ever

L opens the window
cold air shoves into the room
the fire perks up
the hearth glows

he pokes one finger gingerly out
into the falling snow
he has to wait several minutes
before a single crusty flake
floats down and settles
on his fingertip

lying in your house breathing the furred air of night I envisage your beard lifted up over a twoheaded eagle lectern a loud voice ascends from your hidden mouth shaking the rafters   no need to listen too carefully I tell myself burying my head in the pillow's red velvet

the book lies open under your downturned palms *two-ninety-eight* you declare beginning at the beginning with the pencilled price on the flyleaf *copyright nineteen-thirty-six* and so on and on pronouncing each feathery syllable turning the pages thin as skin with their rows of clawmarks which you see as printed words and ciphers

morning snow has bound the house when I bring a lamp to this room already too bright and you still stand there staring over my head at the paintings which have become nothing more than stained blank spaces on the wall   with a sigh you shut the book snap fast the rusted hasp pressing the words and numbers tight against each other in the dark of the closed pages

CRABSEEDS

A man I used to know
Has become my child
One day his mouth grew hard and small
Trying not to let me catch him smiling

From caress of finger
From breathy sticky kiss
He got nothing but a command
To sleep and sleep over
From day to day

Pips in an apple rattle
Like the hurt seeds of his mind
Under his low tread
The fruit breaks and opens
And shells out from sharp capsule
Its small brown stones

Bring me an old plate
And set it under the tree
I want to arrange the crabseeds
So as to resemble
Some kind of disorder

the Celt within
who likes to stand up and sing
ecstatic and undulating songs
is the one who opens my mouth
and lets the lies out
they buzz like a hum of flies
their flight fills the air
with the beat of gauzy strips, and
Angle, that indwelling cousin,
cannot understand
how all the world is listening
says: *verse is a shelter*
of blocks that must be built
carefully for, in the end,
it may become a palace
with electric stars

and together we
walk solitary
by a muddy puddle-edge
(call it a slough)
looking down into water
that returns no reflection
a blank die
shut eye
hidden by the dusk
that creeps up from behind
my shoulders
smoking out of the back trees

not hoping for daylight
not for a long time yet

but at morning
here we come
here I come
cry of throat
and twist of tongue
while it has taken Angle years to build his house
hammering beams and attaching tarpaper
tacking it on so carefully

now the liar, I
stand on the tower
shape the sky
with deceiving fingers
while green damsel flies
on their glassy wings rise
infesting the upper air

Your CHILD
LOOKS *Up*

CLASSIFICATION

One day I went to sleep as a child and next morning awakened as a woman. There I lay in the early light with the fearful knowledge that while I slept, the kingdoms had changed their numbers. The first and the second were the same as always, but the third had become the fifth. How could this have happened, and what strange particles of creation could have pushed their way between?

For answer came the duty angels ascending and descending with amorphous feet the moral ladders of taxonomy, bringing one by one the five volumes of the Book of Divisions and these lay scattered about on the pieced counterpane which covered my knees now so soft and yielding which just last week were knobbly as a boy's.

And I read the confirmation of all my fears, that childhood like a white-whiskered taraxacum seed had taken flight and had floated up into the pale sky until it was lost from my sight, and I thought, one more blessed herb discarded as a weed.

Now everything was changed, damp fog rose from the desert, and the oceans had drained away like bathwater. Nothing remained of them but dry rock and withered strands of algae curling and powdering in the heat.

And I sitting there in my bed following with my finger the letters on the blotched pages of the afterword, all the while my first blood seeping into the white sheet under me.

She told me how it was when I was born
how they took a long knife thin as a leaf
and slashed her up and down and tore
me waxed and silent out of her

"Why Mother why
was I suffocating in the slack flesh of your bowels?
was I stuck in the grip of your stony pelvis?
did I gasp?
did my mouth fill with slime?"

> *"Darling it was the nails of you so sharp*
> *you could have cut five-lane pathways with your feet*
> *It was the head of you so great*
> *You could have burst all my sexy bits*
> *and so they cut me up*
> *and you came out with a bloody head"*

taking my hand in hers to touch the scar
the ropy knotted scar
I felt on her dark belly that ladder thing
to climb up and kiss her smiling face
but *"no"* I said *"no no"*

I laced up my sandal thongs
and got into my dune car
and drove away from her over soft sand
for miles to see the Sphinx

I had to feel how granite meets the sand
and how the ocean touches the shore
I had to fly until my rocket broke
the ceiling of the universe (it was only
hoop paper and burst quite easily)

over my shoulder I shouted to my mother
"tomorrow when I come back be gone
be dead   be buried   be forgotten"'

      "then who will take care of my dust" she whispered

now in the sullen centre of the city
I think of her often   sometimes on seeing old
and austere nuns leaving their house in double file
and their speckly withered hands all woven about
with beads   click click they softly all together
the low musical quaver of their dear old voices
easing away the flesh from the pure calcium
of their most holy bones
                not so my mother with her untrained meat
body boundless   no doubt she leaps up still
distributing her folds less neatly than a manatee
or doesn't she sit somewhere offering to let you
feel her great scar for a dollar?

all haggy she sits in the road
and spits wetly on policemen's trousers
as they drag her sagging bulk towards the wagon

that grimy old whore
will she never keep quiet?

      come Sisters and wash her from sins and spittle
      frock her in blue cotton and set her in the sun
      on a scrubbed wooden chair
      in the kitchen garden

      and teach her how to knit graveclothes
      for the innocent

The gibbous moon in the trees is the head of
a child slipping out between sturdy thighs,
lying under bent and bloodied knees. Every
twig is a coarse hair, pubic, female, innocent.

But the moon is nothing but folded paper, the
Old Man explains, wielding his scissors over
the crisp white sheet, *or a handful of coins,
the quarters one by one pushed into the
slitted back of a pot pig, or maybe a sacred
wafer shoved between the clenched teeth of a
nun.*

Then I told him of when I was brought to bed.
Clouds close-wrapped the body of my child.
They were a net of fine-knotted threads.
Small fingers, small toes kept getting caught
in that web.

The moon wavered in the mist, the wind
moithered like a wailing babe, when the head,
wet as though rained-on, squeezed out through
a slit no bigger than a shrieking mouth.

And the cut rope, and the dark blood
trickling, and the little daughter at last
lying in the lap of the sun.

THE CRANES

The interior sounds the body makes—how do they escape to the outside air, to ears other than our own, though we try to close every orifice? We make sure the eyes are lidded, the ears plugged, the mouth and other sphincters puckered tight. That leaves just the nostrils and they, of course, are continually busy, taking in and pushing out small gulps of air.

And haven't we all heard of the woman whose infant wailed in the womb? She got up to go to him, but could not find him, though she searched the whole house. At last, she remembered he was within her, kicking and crying from the other side of her flesh.

As for me, too late have I resolved to keep myself to myself. Though my fluids may leak out, I'll take nothing more in. The result of this must surely be an inner desert, as arid and gritty as the great sand hills, where in summer cranes walk and call. In autumn, they gather in the dunes and fly south to another desert, even hotter and drier than this one. And somehow, when they return, there is always one left behind, alone as I am, crying out against the solitary fate of females. But why should I need other companions, with this child lying in the crook of my arm, his closed and veiny eyelids, his mouth sealed with a soft white smegma.

How pale he is, barely breathing. There is only just time to awaken him before his sleep slips into an internal state. Before the sound of his cry is lost to this world, and to me who invited him into it.

Halinka

It is right, they say, to bury a stillborn child with a mirror on the pillow beside her. That way, at the resurrection, when she opens her eyes for the first time, she will see her face and recognize herself.

But that's not for you, little daughter, little flaccid creature. For you, there never was such a thing as a face. There were hands and fingers, curled feet with curled toes. There was a heart in your chest, red and whole as a candy, and a white iris growing in the place of your understanding.

the face of the child his simple strength   the faith of his mother who believes he is that inner thing the centre the true hard core   the absurd little garden where he scatters his first seeds the birds believing it's his intention to feed them naturally not breadcrumbs and suet like the old couple next door

his mother imagines a conversation when he asks these neighbours for a few hints on what has gone wrong with his plantation their own yard being a riot of flowers

she finds it difficult not to be disappointed in his lack of every skill but still she believes that one day something will flare in his head and run like fire to his hands

meanwhile she buys nasturtium pods and sunflower seeds thinking these too large for the beaks of song-birds *you have reckoned without the goldfinch* the boy tells her *who can perch on a single reed yet opens these husks making short work of next year's hopes*

then in winter there are mice who never sleep in their tunnels under the snow but run about seeking this morsel and that all night she hears their tiny nibblings which bring her to anxious tears

the son in his mercy looks up at his mother reassuring her that her disillusion will melt away when life rises again from the dirt   *when will that be* she asks but the child whose eyes are hard as nuts won't tell her that

Your Child Looks Up

Your child looks up at you, offers her hand
the empty one

She holds it flat, straight-fingered
every crease outlined in dirt

Dust of the Earth made sticky
with the sweat of effort
a whole afternoon at play

Are you daring enough
to take such a hand

After all where has it been

Stroking caterpillars, probing drains
stirring pond ooze, scratching
her hot little bum

Ah but hasn't she caught you
in your own web of speculation

Just so you won't ask what's
in the other fist hidden
in her drooping knit sleeve

A stallion, an island, an iceberg
a straw hat with green feathers
a train where all the passengers are pigeons

A forbidden book with fine white paper
between glossy colour plates

Don't be so poetic, keep to the prophetic
It's her desire she is hiding

Her desire for the death of her brother
conceived in your bed last night

The Boy At The Upstairs
Window With His Head In His Hands

it is heavy as a stone he tells himself like any rock in the field of
rocks on grandfather's farm where boulders are born out of the
prairie every spring if these are the heads of huge stone infants
where are the bodies to follow narrow from shoulder to toes
after the round agony of the head or could they be ancient
skulls that the earth gives up a thousand years after their burial
what with the rain and the wind something must surely come
to light in the end for this is in many ways the field of jesus the
place where he decided to make an end of his journey he who
had travelled as far as india and back he who has been seen in
every city in the world at one time or another just walking
around stirring up trouble many times thrown into jail for dis-
turbing the peace of such places as this where the bones of the
earth break up and are carried away by farmers who make piles
of them in the corners of every field and dear are these rockpiles
to the child they are his mountains and ramparts and sometimes
he sees brilliant snakes slithering in the cracks the rocks are also
of every colour and grandfather says if you split one of these
suckers you could find a coiled seashell or a perfect fern or per-
haps just a hollow place the boy understands that this hollow is
the very same secret room where he lives always alone tracing
the mysterious maps on the walls with a wetted finger trying to
find how to get away from cartoons of rabbits and cats in hero's
hats to where fair ladies are advertising the subtle gifts of the
mind

The Cloud

A woman is cleaning old hens for the pot. She stands at the kitchen sink looking over a mown paddock, where her son is dawdling his way home from school.

In the low sun blessing his head, she sees a halo of flames consuming his wild shag of hair.

Fright rises in her gullet like a mouthful of mushrooms, perhaps poisonous, perhaps merely inedible.

The boy sits in the grass, knees to chin, picking at the tiny dark dots on his legs. Each one conceals the hidden coil of a hair, ready to erupt as the flake of skin is lifted.

He's thinking of haytime, the swing of his uncle's scythe, the picnic under the hedge, and his mother's voice telling once again the story of when he was three and almost fell down the well.

He's heard it all before, how this field was then a simple pasture, where ancient Edda grazed out her final years. Her only duty was to carry him once a day round the paddock, past the tall copperbeech to the door of the house and his mother's arms. That last time, the old donkey missed her footing on the slippery scatter of empty masts, tossed him to the very brink of the open well.

If, his mother keeps saying, *you had been one pound heavier. If Agnes had not been standing there, winching up a bucketful.* But he cannot remember the incident.

Of the animal he recalls only weathered droppings, fading year by year into the litter behind the broken leanto, until they disappeared.

Tonight he decides, he will ask to camp out in the paddock; the old shed can be his tent.

That mildewed place, his mother will say, and she'll hand him a sooty kettle. *Better make a fire, brew up. You could catch something.*

The very words she'd said that other time in town, when he'd stopped to speak with a grey labouring man warming his hands over a brazier, where two ashy potatoes roasted side by side in the failing embers. *As sure as eggs is eggs,* she'd said, pulling him away, *you could catch something. It's easy done.*

Now she's emptying the last bird, pulling the trail from the scratchy hollow of the carcass, watching the child get up from the grass and run toward the house. *Mother, Mother,* he's shouting.

She doesn't answer, sees only the blistered arms, the trouser legs neatly pinned over the stumps of thighs, her own trembling hand carrying a spoonful of porridge to the helpless mouth.

She drops the spoon into the empty bowl, then rummages in the dresser drawer for a strong white comb, begins the slow untangling of his hair.

The Varying Hare

(We shall not all sleep, but we shall all be changed—CORINTHIANS 1:52)

a prayer for the child going to bed
a prayer for his departing
holding in his right hand the enamel
candlestick white with a chipped blue rim
grasping in his left the hem
of his worn nightgown
so as not to fall on the stairs

his brother is allowed to sleep in his clothes
rumpled as they are for fear he may get up at night
and catch his death wherever he can find it

this prayer the mother says to the little one
is simply a defence against creatures
who live at the end of the world
whose snares are like satan's

the child dreams of a rabbit
he dreams his father catches it
with a single looped strand of wire

the big brother lies on his cot
thinking of knowledge got in school
tested in the forest
thinking of himself sitting
at an old oak desk carved with the noble names
of those who long ago marched off to war

his father has told him how they were led away
not to be seen again   probably
they are out there still stepping it
over hill and through marsh

their boots never leaving a print
on wet ground or dry

father the boy says *open the book*
where it tells of the snowshoe hare
her brown coat tipped with white
how lovely she is leaping
and foraging all night
her colours made chalky by the moon
her wary eye on the shadow of an owl

mother the boy writes *it is dawn*
and I have gone into the forest
to visit the hare in her thorny and snowy set
where she sleeps concealed by a tangle
of rose and red osier
god knows nothing can keep her
from the various predators
whose prey she is

tomorrow she may change as we all must
to scrap fur in a tattered bundle

up to now I have told you only the tales of my wanderings hith-
er and thither across this earth   journeys are all the same I pack
the same clothes in the same pigskin bag I've had since age sev-
enteen   down in the kitchen I open a drawer rummaging for
plastic sacks for my shoes then I wash my hair check my keys
and I'm off   two days later I'm to be found at amy's or jack's or
peter's sometimes it is australia or chile sometimes france or
maryland once it was bulgaria scented with rose attar   next
morning I awaken to birds there is a mist or there is none a
horse stands with his head over a gate his feet in grass which is
neither short nor long he's not my grey but a roan or chestnut
with a starred forehead who doesn't whinny at my approach
some will nuzzle for apples but it's a fool thing to trust a
stranger   I raise my hand and the horse shies off

now honny be still and listen to the various stories of my stay-
ing home because for your sake that's what I shall do from now
on   I fill an old basin with water *here* I say *play with this* and I
drop in a handful of walnut shells which float away on their sep-
arate voyages to the other side of the basin where a sunken
world of chipped enamel stained with yellowish rust shows
beneath the ripples *nothing at all grows in that land* I suggest *it's
a cold desert where devils live   none but the brave men of walnut
dare set foot upon that icy shore*

and so it goes   every now and then I must stop and think of
something to amuse the moment so that you won't notice the
pain of the story the tediousness of the telling   you are biting
your lip again let's carry out the papers those battered cartons of
dusty ledgers and journals that sit on every couch and chair
we'll march them down to the burning barrel and put a match
to the lot   grey paper ash flies out floating and settling catch-
ing at the twigs of the leafless hedge I brush flakes of it from my
jacket from your fuzz of white hair and I look into your eyes
those vague moons dampened by smoke

later I begin the story of the little bureau how once I tried to compress my meaning into its rosewood pigeonholes and drawers how I locked my letters away with a brass key small as a clock key it's lost now and the letters lie there still smelling of mildew and body powder the folded sheets of blue paper crossed and recrossed in my awkward hand when I put my ear to the keyhole I can hear them puffing out the envelopes then drawing them in *huff-puff* a sound not as loud as mice   of course I meant to mail them sometimes but by now the people have moved away grown old and died at other addresses *the chimneys* I remember and *filly's corner* and *66 ellerton sussex* and a farm in normandy suitably named *les vaches*

you are growing restless again honny let me give you a drawer of your own to play with a very tiny one pulled from our grandmother's dressing table be careful it's heavy for its size made of dark mahogany the handle a filigree knob   inside are short pieces of edging lace and a tangle of narrow satin ribbons three crinkled hairpins lie beneath the ribbons they are the sort old women used to wear in their yellowy-white upswept braids

at once grandmother appears in her seventieth year she has had her hair shingled and permed and faintly blued it shines unnaturally against the crochet-edged pillow in the enormous bed   I am twelve years old and expected to be dutiful in my neat kilt and knitted kneesocks I find myself walking to the bottom of the bed where there is a blue velvet *chaise longue* in place of the usual trundle I lie down and wait for orders *shut your eyes child* says the familiar complacent voice grandmother presses the bell beside the pillow she orders the servant to bring me a shetland blanket and a glass of hot milk *I must be ill* I tell myself my spirits rising for what if I'd been in disgrace grandmother has decided I am ill what heavenly relief not to have to decide that for myself   I drift off into a feverish sleep   after a while she rings again this time for her maid willis to take my temperature in the chagrin of your boredom you have torn the ribbons to shreds wait now I'll find something else for you to do and I hand you the gold-nibbed fountain pen from the nightstand grandmother kept it there always at hand for the sacred duty of writing her household cheques   *now we come to the really boring part* I say distinctly so that you cannot accuse me of springing tedium upon you without warning but you don't hear me are staring solemnly at your fingers as they pull the pen apart long ago the ink has dried in the patent suction tube nothing remains but a faint blue iridescence on the tiny pieces of perished rubber which you scatter around your feet   that didn't last long

as I drone on explaining what made me come home and stay home to care for your strange whims and piques I'm casting about for some further distraction for I must have you sit here and listen while I tell you the rest of the story

The woman who lived alone on the edge of the moor looked up one morning from her sewing and her cup of clover tea. Had she imagined that sound something between a child singing and the yip of a fox? Had she imagined that skipping shadow crossing the pathway that led into the woods beyond the garden?

It was not like the shadow of a wolf or a bear or any of the other wild creatures she saw quite often moving amongst the trees. Sometimes these were friendly and sometimes they were menacing. She knew them all by sight and did not disturb their lives nor they hers.

But this presence was of a different kind, and she waited to see what or who approached her house. But the shadow flitted away and was gone amongst the trees.

Next day, and the day after that, the woman saw the shadow again but still she had not seen the creature who owned it. On the third day, however, when she looked up from her work, she saw a young boy standing there on the pathway. He was thin as a deer, and his hair hung raggedly down about his shoulders like the mane of a wolf. He was naked as a nestling, and his eyes were like the eyes of a hawk seeking its prey.

The woman called out to the child who, at the sound of her human voice, immediately vanished into the woods. But still after that he came every day to her dooryard, and she fed him birdseed and chopped roots and gave him goat's milk to drink.

Time passed and the boy became a little more friendly. On nights of sharp frost he even came into the house to sleep. Not that he would lie in a bed. He slept on a pile of straw in the corner furthest from the stove, for it was obvious that he was mortally afraid of the fire.

As the weeks and the months went by, the woman and the boy became accustomed to one another. She cut his hair neatly around his head and every evening she called him to sit at her feet while she combed out the knots and the tangles and the burrs and the twigs. She took his measure and made him a rough country smock and breeches. She even taught him to say a few words in his strange voice which was like the cry of a raucous bird, but he was never able to tell her who he was or how he came to live wild in the forest.

As for his eyes, they were piercing as a pigeonhawk's, and indeed some afternoons he went into the woods and caught rabbits or small birds for the pot. When the woman found these offerings laid at her feet, as though by a faithful hound, she skinned and plucked them and even managed to teach her wild boy which herbs to bring from the garden to add to the stew. She would sit down at the table to eat with a napkin laid across her knee, but he took his portion into the yard and devoured it straight from the gravely dirt, without benefit of even so much as a tin plate. As she daintily cut the meat from the bones she tried to forget the toothmarks at the throat of the prey. And so she named the boy Ferret, and that was the name he would answer to when she called him to her.

A year passed and the wild boy and the quiet woman got used to one another. In fact she had almost begun to think of him as her son. But that was not to last. One spring day he simply disappeared into the woods and did not return. When dusk fell she walked a little way among the trees calling his name. There was no sign of him that night, or the next, and when she found the clothes she had made for him dropped in a heap on the back doorstep, she knew in her heart that her feral boy had gone back to the wild and would never return to her.

Once more she was left to her solitary pursuits of sewing and sweeping and baking and brewing tea. Mornings, as she sat in her window, she would glance up every so often at the garden and the forest beyond, hoping, yet not daring to hope, for one more glimpse of that shadow on the dirt path, longing to hear once more that strange cry, something between a howl and a song.

I

grandmother has a mouth
like a crinkled O

    oh she says continuing the story
    the princess was beautiful
    and all her clothes were samite
    and reached to the floor
    only when she walked could you see
    her feet creeping in and out
    like mice from the shelter
    of her skirt
    her hands were gloved
    with the rings on the outside
    so that the prince could kiss them
    and not touch her delicate fingers
    her mouth was reddened
    her cheeks rouged
    her face was veiled in a gauzy mist
    of silkysheen facepowder

    I have been selling it for years dear
    I am the sole agent for this part of the country
    when you grow up sweetheart
    you shall be one of my salesladies
    we'll measure you for silk veils
    and underthings and bouquets
    you want to be a princess
    don't you darling?

II

granny your mouth is planted with rue and artemesia
the bitter herbs of the last meal
when you speak you chew on them
and tears come to your eyes
wrinkles ray from your blue eyes
squinted against the sun   your arms
are stained with brown flecks
you cannot wear makeup it would slide like rain
from your tanned face   it would fall as dust
into the dust of the prairie
your hands have become crooked on the washboard
the nails are split
your shoulders are shrubby branches
your breasts hang down like chokecherries
around your cunt grow stiff prairie plants
whose withies are tough
whose leaves are aromatic
they flower orange red yellow as locoweed
as buffalobean   some have fleshy roots like tumours
that cause you to walk sideways in the fall
they will not flower for the first five years
after that they will blossom for fifty seasons
or so your mother told you
when you were little yourself
in another place in another time
reading in a book with fine glossy
illustrations about princesses
your father came into the nursery
kissed your glossy curls
lifted you in his arms
smelled your little tot smell
he brought you a rose from the garden
he cut off the thorns
with his pearl-handled penknife

III

and now you and I grandmother
take old kitchen knives and a basket
to dig roots on the sunny side
of the valley hills   how iron-hard
is the dirt   my knife breaks
at the handle but you know better
have lugged a pail of water
you pour it round the plant
after a while you begin to dig
the root of the psoralea is huge
is succulent   we spit
the hard fibres into our hands
after dinner you light a lamp
you bring out your sewing
the silky goods stick to your rough fingers
the fine threads snag   you want to sew
me a dress with three ruffles
you want to stitch me underwear
of silk and lace   you hold the gauzy
stuff against the light
the flowery print pales
but I want a floursack nightgown
like the one you are wearing in the picture
taken outside the soddy in nineteen-ten
with molly and ted the new team
hitched to a wide harrow
the nightgown is embroidered around the yoke
around the hem   your mother did it
with floss from the pedlar
she did it in the shack
while the men were out hauling wood

IV

the spine of the book is broken
it is mended with tape
the coloured plates keep falling out
the princess in the picture
holds out her hand
to the kneeling prince
he is wearing crimson velvet kneebreeches
and a powdered wig
her hair is a golden tower
her glass shoes are small as mice
her eyes are blue and shrewd
there is a sweet smile on her lips

GREY-EYED FRANCES

people are always asking me:
do you have children?
is your mother still living?

what they mean is:
have you a husband?
are you alone in your bed?

I have had this photograph taken
of my mother and myself
my daughter
and her daughter

we three women are smiling
but the child is gravely staring
out of her dark corner
over the drooping posy
of washed-out cloth violets
she is holding

small Frances
grey-eyed Frances
she is sometimes spiteful
always forgiving

I am wrapping the picture
to send to an old lover of mine
someone I haven't heard from
in ten years

I am doing it out of spite
it has nothing to do with love

the river
where I learned to swim
has become a dry bed
other lakes and streams
are full to the edges I notice

there was a low rumble
and then the earth caved in
and the water poured down
to the core of our world

homeward I walk
between the wooded banks
as though our river
was nothing but a sunken road

dragonflies hover
above the rank weeds
hemlock and sowthistle
taller than a woman
where slowfin chub
made our floats bob
on saturday mornings

and under the broken tilt
of the wooden swingbridge
are two mossy jamjars
one of them cracked
the other holds the husk
of a papery crayfish

but where are the bones
of Daisy Filman
who was drowned just here
when I was twelve years old?

this is my lament
composed for that occasion
I am squatting on grey planks
singing it again

I remember you well Daisy
your long feet and eyes of hazel
you died of love
poor Daisy Filman
when your soldier married
that girl from Winchester

my third, the red-haired one (isn't it natural that I've forgotten her name after so many years) was delicate from the start

afraid that some evil would carry her away from me, I was always plotting to protect her   every morning I made her stand naked beside her bed while I examined her body for warts and moles and cracks between the toes, for I feared her vitality might leak out through these little imperfections   when I found the slightest scratch I covered it with sticking plaster cut into a tiny circle it was lightest pink, paler even than her own skin

at bedtime while she knelt on a cushion beside my chair reading aloud from her primer I searched the roots of her long red hair for lice I combed and combed with a finetooth ivory comb I had never seen a louse but imagined them slender and brown with pincers at their heads something like very small earwigs

as I combed I felt a sick dread closing my throat for I knew that armies of these creatures could rise up without warning from my daughter's rosy scalp for were they not waiting somewhere beyond sight to attack her from the shimmering ambush of her own hair?

she had the pale thin legs and protruding belly of a child who is never quite well   of course she was not an active girl yet how quick she was with her tongue how glib how sharp   she could never bear to eat fish I could see it made her ill even to think of it   on fridays she was not herself sat silent and tense at table   as soon as she was certain that no one was watching she dropped the offending food into the white napkin spread across her knees then she excused herself and slipped out into the hallway where there was a tank of great yellow carp   I could hear a slight splash as she rolled the fillet deftly from the napkin what made her so sure that fish would eat fish? they did of course   they darted at her offering in a multiple flash of gold then opened their silly red-lined mouths and gobbled down the white or pink flakes   when all was eaten the child dabbled her fingers in the water and scrubbed them dry on the cleanest corner of the napkin

one friday she looked up and saw me watching her through the arch of the doorway   in the greenish cloud of her glance I read both pleading and rebellion   deciding it was easier to accept her weakness than challenge her strength I turned away without a word

my dear child
how small you have grown
how slender the fingers that fiddle
along the fine strings of your hair
and your eyes which used to be
huge sky reflectors have shrunk
to the size of wild green hazels
pushed into your head
behind the drooping lids

      ready to go?
      ready to go
      the deadheads all
      picked off
      the lawn mown
      to the quick
      the washing
      all taken down
      and folded away
      in a basket

the hot bus pants and squawks to a stop
your feet are yellowing birchleaves
skittering down the porch steps

I stretch out my hand
rather rough and scaly
like the claw of an old hen
scratching for a kernel
not even as big as a grain of wheat

you are a winged weedseed
smaller than a flake of dust
a mote that catches in
the driver's eye

NETTLES

When I am old
I will totter along broken pavements
the strings of my boots undone
smelling a bit strong like any
fat old woman who has forgotten
which day is Tuesday
(my bath night if you like)

stiff my clothes from old dirt
not sweat at my age mumbling
the cracked enamel mug

eleven cats playing
in my weedy yard drinking
my little ration of milk
with me   and withy withy
the cats circle around my house
at night singly filing
in and sleeping on the
saggy stained bed and the chair
and the crumby tabletop

One day they will find me dead
O dead dead
A stinking old bundle of
                        dead

and in my hand
a peeled wand
and in my ear a cricket sitting
telling me stories and predictions

and the time of night

Childermas Three

one Sunday in May our children
who have hardly noticed us till now
decide on a Feast of Recognition

the youngest brings chains of withering marigolds
twines them over the backs of our chairs
the two eldest, with napkins over their arms,
bring in the dinner course by course
the food, thank goodness, is invisible
we gesture over huge empty plates
our daughter, not spilling a drop,
pours red ink into the glasses for wine

the last course is a much more solemn affair
we are told to rise and all together sing

the muddled singing gives a mewling sound

then a dish of flames is set down before me
its cinders glowing like cherries
you are luckier
get a basket of petals
into which you dip your face
making munching noises

you come up smiling
crushed petals cling to your hair

who is to blame for my lips' blisters?

afterwards your cool mouth
tastes of almonds

DESIRE

As So Many Do

The day starts bright as a songbird. Later, it turns grey and begins to drip. Wings of clouds mantle the town where melancholy grass is beginning to turn yellow at the roots.

It was a day like this I had a fit of grief on the bus so that my tears wriggled down my face like rain on window glass. The man behind me tapped me on the shoulder, offered a blue cotton handkerchief. The woman beside me dug in a damp paper bag and handed me one of those sugared doughnuts that are so gritty and hard to swallow.

Afterwards, I noticed I had accepted the young man's arm. I leaned on him as we walked homeward, his shoulder wet with my sorrow. Or was it simply the drizzle dampening every surface?

When we reached the house I wouldn't let him go, and so he sat down beside me on the bed limply smoking. After a while, we both dozed off, bundled and sinless as I thought then.

I awoke to find he had taken off with several of Harry's things, which were still lying about the house—a pair of pigskin gloves, two antiquarian books, and a black silk umbrella.

Now he might have needed the brolly, but what could he possibly want with rare books, a man I didn't even know the name of. I made enquiries. He wasn't a local boy.

On dark afternoons like this, I open the curtains wide and sit obviously reading under the soft light of the lamp. Surely the rain will return that stranger to me, he of the cool consoling hand, he of the light fingers.

desire is not like a wedding which rushes relentlessly towards us from the other end of time   it comes unexpected as a cloud inviting questions and implying answers   *can three lovers meet as two* we ask   can they walk out of a summer's morning and roll as all true lovers must in the dewy wayside grass without one of them feeling neglected, worse still pitied, by the other two   can four lovers meet as three or must they remain always two pairs as isolated from each other as we all are from the begetter of our uncertainties   and does all this apply not only to lovers but to brothers and sisters both secular and holy

darling we shall say to our child *you were born of our surprising ability to couple and couple again without weariness without a thought for the garden half-planted for the book half-read* certainly we shall never tell her of our present condition what an effort it is to keep up an interest for the sake of our tinpot relationship for the sake of our parenthood for the sake of the future which while we lie here locked in each other is rapidly crumbling into the past

you find yourself waiting at an unfamiliar crosswalk beside a man in swimtrunks with a washed-out towel flung across his shoulders his feet shoved into sloppy sandals at first you think he hasn't noticed you then *out for a swim ducks* he asks in a low but distinct voice   you are dressed rather splendidly in a tight satin dress and very high heels with bows also a straw hat and crochet gloves but you nod anyway prepared to follow this one wherever he goes

it's a long walk and he's difficult to keep up with as he strides along down streets round corners over bridges and past church-es until at last he stops in front of an enormous building if you can call it that for there's no roof simply a high brick wall enclosing a whole city block   from inside comes a low mur-muring as of a great cloud of insects settling down to sleep

an earnest-looking boy is working away washing slogans from the bricks scrubbing out the white words with a longhandled broom which he dips from time to time into a pail full of what smells like a mixture of piss and turpentine you want to hold your nose and run but manage not to as you can tell by their attitudes that neither the boy nor the man will stand for such behaviour

what a relief when mr swimtrunks takes you by the hand and leads you slowly and gently round the outside of the strange enclosure but search as you may neither of you can see the slightest sign of a door or a window in the endless brick barrier the whole thing seems hopeless until on the third time around you notice that the boy has left taking the pail with him but leaving his broom and his rickety wooden ladder propped up against the wall now's your chance   the man goes up first of course and sits astride the wall describing the scene below as a vast artificial lake made from layers and layers of bluegreen plastic with excellent designs of weeds and fishes painted upon it   you kick off your shoes and clamber up   when you reach the top and sit down beside him you point out that he's forgotten to mention the cutout paper swimmers surging about in the exhaust from twenty or so vacuum cleaners each one pushed by a respectable lady in a housedress, the twenty heads covered with twenty rayon kerchiefs   you can tell by the lumps that they are all wearing curlers something even your mother gave up long ago

by now your man is standing wobble-footed on the wall ready to dive in for the promised swim and you beside him with your arms stretched upwards regarding the plastic water with fear and hate but it's too late to change your mind and you're deter- mined to float down with him through the hum   just then the women turn off their machines with one simultaneous click and there you are in the silence between sky and plastic longing for that beloved voice *out for a swim ducks* he'll say and if he does- n't you'll pretend he has just to feel that ultimate rush of love up your tired legs

It Wasn't A Major Operation

the surgeon joined us
with a long wire he threaded
through your left earhole
and into my right one

when we woke up from the anaesthetic
we had to begin practicing at once
every time you nodded your head
I inclined mine
we bobbed together this way and that

when the wire was too taut
there was a knotted feeling in my head
when it was too slack
it looped and caught in my necklace

but now we have got used to
the continual lolling motion
and are able to go
for a short walk every day

this morning while we were
admiring the lilies
a row of birds sat down on our wire

night has fallen now
and they are still here
nine sparrows and a kingbird

ERGOT AND AFTER

We were standing on the grass breathing
not even the first word had been spoken
when a great mushroom jumped out of the grass
between us and obscured the trees and the horizon
and the utter blue

Where is your grace O Lord that you
should root my love in such shallow soil
like the bush on the Shield
where every tree falls down
after ten years' growth

"look at that" I said to my love
"our love is a mushroom as tall as a tower
the towers of drowned cities
were once as tall as this thing between us"

Come peel the pithy stem
come cut the gray-pink flesh
it is good for us to drink
the juice that trickles from
the torn side of the Lamb
and don't pass up this opportunity
to save Save SAVE
at the great Precambrian post-Christian sale

cry out and say
"we have come to rescue all mushrooms from Campbell's cans"
cream is pouring over them
and I could spray on you
the ultimate in deodorants my mate
why should we smell of mating
when the cry is exterminate
all creepy-crawlies and live

in a grassy Eden alone with you
and detergents to wash the stones of the waterfall
and no more moss

The moss was green and underneath
crept mycelium and worms
twisted together in leafmold
and rotting corpses
now let me rot and nourish your shallow roots
why embalm me when all has fallen to dust
and ashes are in our mouths
let's cut our way into this fungus
and live in a house edible and earthy
or shall we burn up what God saw
when he pushed the C button for the stars
to bubble and burst against his thighs

he knows
you know   I know
what swells in love
what we want is to erupt spray and expand
into a universe

Shall we burn our mushroom to a cloud of smoke?

or shall we dig holes and spawn fungus between the planets?

and between you and me my love
some sort of truce
to prevent murder

It's over you know, the summer's over.
Clouds of dust as the last vehicle went out.

A jeep hauling a small boat on a trailer
Through the dust of the grey country road.

Patterns of tires, patterns of cast leaves
Printed in ashen dust

The next day clouds of snow, the crumbled sky
Falling and settling on the trees
Of the bare abandoned forest.

They have all returned to the city, while I remain
Sorting my summer notebooks:

Drawings of tender plants begun in the spring
Pressings of leaves

Which are prints of tough early autumn, before
The rot comes that thickens
The floor of the woods.

And what lies beneath the snow, the needle duff?
Cities of pebbles and crushed shells,

Kingdoms of beetles, republics of worms,
Forests of hyphae, tangled mycelium,

Roots of trees coming upon each other
In the dark.

The question is always the same:
Did you decide to leave me,
Or did I decide to remain here alone?

And what is alone? A white sky,
An empty hill, a forest without leaves?

A house with one chair, one cup
One bent knife, a narrow bed,
One coat on one peg.

From the first day I knew I must begin
To talk to myself, for fear of forgetting

The sound, the use of words.
For fear that for me they would become

Mere bird-scratches on paper,
Botanist's Latin on a page of notes.

When a word describes, tell me does it become
The thing described? Is distance itself

The sound of the word—*distance, distance?*

Wherever you are, why don't you
Turn and look back across that distance,

And see the ocean stretching, and the land,
Mountainous, and flat,

And see the forest
Where we were together.

Tell me, what is a forest
But so many single trees

Each clattering its bony branches in the wind,
Each standing among its fallen companions.

On Singleness

Today I've become for the first time a lonely woman,
A lonely woman in a woollen skirt and shawl

Moving heavily from one room to another,
Back and forth from the bedroom to the kitchen,

From the kitchen to the storeroom.
I've become someone deciding what to do next,

While the daylight lasts;
What to do next

While the oil lasts for the lamp,
The logs for the stove.

In the crock a half-loaf, in the cupboard/cheese
Wrapped in its vinegared muslin,

Two tins of corned beef on the shelf,
In the back of the store five jars

Of lakefish, two of riverfish, berries and
Berries, then mushrooms:

Twenty jars pickled and eleven jars dried,
A small sack of wheat, when opened
Smells softly of mould,

And salt in a block like cattle salt.

I count everything over and over.
I wipe the tops of the jars

I murmur *that's all, that's all.*
I have become an old woman

With cold hands counting jars.
That's all, that's all.

And later out with the maul
To split wood, the last of the wood

That we sawed in the last of the summer.
The block rings like a stone struck.

Shivers of snow fall from the branches.
Above me the usual raven sits in the naked tree,

Croaking his dry claim to my answer.
My dark companion I tell him,

*After the logs are split, after the kindling
Is chopped into white slivers,*

*I shall come with my chipped enamel dishpan
And gather clean snow,*

Being careful to keep away from
The bird tracks, the mouse seed,
The rabbit scat.

My wife left me
When we were both quite young
She said she was going to visit her cousin
There must have been more to it than that

Last summer she came back
Just before harvest
I awoke and she was there
Baking pies in our wedding dishes

She's a grey and folded woman now
Even her lips are creased
But sometimes when she sits there phoning
A curve of her cheek or arm
Reminds me of the girl she once was

What good is that to me?
I want to remember her always
As she is now

BERTHA

Lully my bitch is
Licking strangers' hands these days
I loved her but she wanted
Green shelters and town houses
With air-conditioned stairs
"A maid arranging irises in
Tall vases is worth all the words
You pay out George and more"

What she doesn't know is that
I keep my old withered wife
Below stairs ready to take me over
When I get tired of bitty skirt
And big titty

My white wife I haven't looked
At you for years   perhaps
Your watery eyes are still blue
Deep in their baggy sockets

for T.H.

a world in the shape of an egg
lies in the palm of the hand

which warms it and the warmth
brings out the sheen of the eggshell

you stare at its wholeness which you know
is present only from moment to moment

in your other hand in a nest of worn fingers
lies another egg which you see as exactly like

the first but the fingers know the difference
for this one is withdrawn from its chalky shell

into its chill yolk   cannot
be warmed at a touch

god hold me to myself you cry out departing
not comprehending how you will pass through

that wall thin as eggshell to where
everything seems exactly as it was at home

yet there is a difference
if only you could put your hand on it

in the morning the farmwife comes from the house
her apron full of wheat

or what passes for wheat until the sun
hits it and it sparkles   handfuls

of crystals thrown up never to fall
while the silly hens gobble at nothing

and the young woman erased for a moment
by the dazzle of the sun

turns and becomes that other girl
rosy and solid whom you left years ago

Hanner Hwch Hanner Hob— The Flitch

huw from the mountain lover of pigs
comes down for the kill
he who loves truly says huw kills

and he so quiet when he says it
the pig looking up at him
from her little gilt eyes
so you're the one too small to be a mother
says he to the pig called nancy
I can see she trusts him to make
something good of her a useful chine
and sausage   coils of black pudding
beside jellied feet and brawn in the larder

nancy nancy says huw jones
I've made a bed for you see
it's all new straw sweet hay strewn about
lie down my love my beauty lie down *fach*
he says it in welsh of course
how many pigs understand english after all?

and he tells her the tale of the first hogs
how pryderi got them from the lord of ireland
how he kept them styed in the south
how math king of dyfed sent the bard gwydion
to steal them away with his storytelling
his magic and trickery

how the men of the south pursued gwydion
and saturday morning there was a great battle
all because of the pigs see
and when math and his warriors
were bloodying and brawling at the fight

goewin the king's footmaiden was violated
well you wouldn't want that to happen to you
says huw to nancy
the gilt's not so sure she wouldn't
well then darling says huw
and he takes out his sharp little pigknife
and sticks her one
she's gone in a minute
with one happy sigh

when he sees me watching from the pony stall
I could do the same for you *fach* says huw
if I'd just had that much blessing
to be born a pig I tell him
I wouldn't mind it at all

two young women are walking arm in arm up the highstreet they work in a shoe factory and have just got their first pay-checks now they are off to the shops to buy skirts and cardigans of loganberry wool knit also some gauzy underwear and stock-ings and other falderals   they are chatting and laughing as they go for they are very good friends and never tire of one another's company

a man rides by on his bike   as he passes the two friends he can't resist turning his head for another look for they are such a charming pair with their shining hair and teeth and their stur-dy legs in flesh-coloured stockings

it would be a shame the young man thinks to court and marry one of them and take her away from her mate then both of them would be unhappy for who would find time to chat so amiably about the diets they were on or about the courses they were planning to take at the technical institute

what I should do he decides *is to fly away with both of them to the south seas* there we could all live together in a grass hut by the seashore the girls can chat all day as they pick breadfruit and deck each other's hair with hibiscus blossoms

and he's happy too   every day he fishes in the lagoon every night he lies between the two friends on a soft mattress of palm fronds whichever way he turns there is always a lovely young thing ready to greet him with open arms

all the same a man can get to feel trapped by a life like this   could he for instance ever get away without their noticing   well he must just wriggle ever so carefully to the bottom of the bed and escape without waking either of them and so one night he creeps quietly out of the grass hut and hails a passing ship which takes him back to the murky north   there he finds a job in a factory making small engine parts

each morning he gets up very early and makes himself a piece of toast and a cup of tea then he wheels his bicycle out of the shed and rides off to work through the dark deserted streets

IN PRAISE OF MY OWN BREASTS

And why, you ask, do I have this bosom like a shelf. You mean a shelf of land, shading the water at the base of a cliff. The sea has eaten what's underneath as the tide comes and goes swallowing chalk and flints.

It's not like that. I think this bust is a thicket of sharp thorns, yet brave birds do make their nests here. They bring soft hay and the blond hair of young nuns when it's time to cast off their novitiate, at Lammas when they make their final vows. The leaves of the breasttree shelter the chicks from rain and it's warm here close to the heart of things.

And I've had it said that my breasts are twin puddings stirred by the hand of God. That is when he gets up to his old tricks in the fall. The pudding cloth covers sweet plums and spices, come Christmas will the cloths burst as they did last year in the boiling?

A lover told me one breast is a giant puffball the other a coconut. One is full of sweet milk the other of ripe spores. He didn't say which he admired the most. Another fellow whittled them down, one to a sweet pippin the other to a sour baking apple. I didn't invite him in to do the cooking.

I'm getting old and they've softened now, a mouse family or a small swarm of bees could hide behind these things, but they're not finished yet. I've heard you can make two wallets from any dead granny's dugs. Me, when I go I'll bequeath you a couple of saddle bags, capacious and serviceable, lined with soft feathers and green leaves. Fastened with hooks and eyes.

Ah the cliff edge—where so many murders are done
Can't you see the body among the boulders
Far down on the beach?
While seagulls scream they are filming
A frail girl in a thin nightgown
Prone on the distant rocks

Mr. B and I are walking hand in hand
Up the cliff path knowing
That under our feet
Disaster and drama are making a second-rate movie
Take no notice my darling Mr. B
Tell me a simple answer to the urgent question
Who am I?   Who are we?

Mr. B is a known madman   a suspected murderer
I think the cops are after him for being himself
For not sobbing
For not beating his breast
When he finds a victim on the beach
Bloody and wet in the tide
Was that my body we saw down there Mr. B
Twisted in seaweed   Who am I?   Who was I?

He picked me up on the beach

I am the tiny girl in the thin nightgown
That Mr. B carries in a seashell
In his trousers pocket among
The sticks of Dentyne gum and the spent flashbulbs
Oh I'm glad I'm dead and can't see
The dirty darkness in here

I was murdered last Thursday but even so
The heat of his groin
And all the fumbling that goes on there
Is disturbing my final rest

Hats are in and on our next visit to town we each buy three of them. Then we get our cousin Aden, the one that's as old as an uncle,

to whittle us hat stands—mine painted black and Helen's white. The stands have branches that stick up like candelabra.

The rule is we're to start with the middle hat, then go to the right and then the left.

The next Sunday we begin to wear our hats. Helen bows her head and moves her lips in prayer to the God of finery, to the God of flighty young girls.

The two golden pheasant quills in her green felt poke into the back of a young man sitting in front of her. He turns his head and loves her instantly. Thus was her prayer answered.

My hat is a soft straw full of buds and flowers. I have sprinkled it with rosewater to make it smell real. As I sit there with my hymn-book in my gloved hand, I hear the buzzing of Mr. Cox's bees.

I pray to God that they don't crawl into my ears and make a hive of my head. Through the hum of the bees I hear the Vicar say, "All things in creation speak to us, and we should listen." But how difficult to understand are the intentions of bees,

these creatures said to be wise above all others, that belong to us but only at their discretion.

Next day I take my three hats down to Cox's. I offer them to the bees in repentance for my vanity. And the queen accepts my gift and sends two of her people to light on my earlobes and tell me their secrets of pollen and of wax and even of nectar. But not of course the secret of honey, that they keep to themselves.

Helen and her lover are kissing in the bushes. They are laughing at my ceremony, but what do I care. In the end all of us must find out about that thing that's between a man and a woman.

But I know the secrets of bees, their flights, their dances, how they are fierce but forgiving, how they take our human measure and make us all slaves to their sweetness.

EARLY SORROW

it happened in Saskatoon
where the sky is high and
the brass sun over the bridge
is shaking in the heat
and I am walking with the girl
with the oriental eyes

look how she leaves tracks
wild tacks in the dust of her footprints
her toenails need cutting and I say
"dear let me cut them" but
"they might bleed" she says

I wish my seed had settled in her
secret place but I cannot see myself
holding the child's hand
a child with blue slant eyes
red frizz top and feet that don't match?
and Oh hell why didn't I?

that was the day she came with me to the park
they all came and sat down elbow to elbow
in the long grass eating
out of each other's pockets
love love we sang quietly all together
crushing the weeds with wet sounds
blowing out smoke between our clenched teeth

but I watch my girl as she sets down
her small brown silky lotus bum
among the dandelions
darling cross your legs
so that ants won't crawl in that honey crack
I am to be bee and not that melancholy Spaniard

who beckons with stained fingers
he calls her away with fingers on the strings
and sound moves   it jumps and clicks
on the rings of his fingers

night it alone shall I?
shall I send on her few small folded panties
gold thongs of her broken sandals?
shall I send her a cheerful letter wherever she is
gone from one hand to the other
or still with the Spaniard's
stained fingernails breaking
the skin of those olive thighs

small price of a stamp
I could have mailed myself through that slit
but no I am a hollow boy   hollow as a guitar
and without strings to tie my parcel

Stopover

our airport is small and grubby
you have to wait a long time for your luggage

     you say you are in love

if you are in love
why do you pull your hair back like that
why do you tie it so tightly
away from your forehead?

you are taller than I remember
were you not once a small woman
thin and introverted
in a sharp and willful way

and you keep looking into the distance
and you keep saying

     "this must be
     this has to be
     some sort of a beginning"

I break my comb in two
I put the pieces together
back to back
they are the teeth of a face I once knew
black teeth dirty at the roots
reminding me that wild creatures
eat each other
hair and bones and all

lend me a couple of cigarette papers dear
I'm going to play you a song
to welcome you home to the prairies

"your lover lies
his tongue is twisted
your lover lies with you
your tongue is twisted too"

you stare and stare
through the dusty glass walls
while I rub shredded paper from my lips

A Game Of Angels

Look at me I say
to your face on the pillow
to your eyes with their straight glossy stare

I move my arms up and down to remind you
that I am that woman who once came
with armfuls of ferns, with armfuls
of branches, bunched them and
pinned them to the shoulders
of your tunic, trying to persuade you
to flap and fly upwards
out of this cup of earth
between the mountains

Remember I say
those sundays we spent
in a tent of sheets
testing our hold on each other
caressing with silky pinions
one another's flesh
      how our mouths' soft beaks
 gave off cries like battling doves
or other fierce creatures

The eagle for instance
flying upwards
until the sun irked our watching eyes
as it flashed between
those specks of wings

When the bird fell
on gopher or prairie mouse
we could hear the air
whistling through its claws
and you smiled

As you do now
grasping the blankets
with old talons

PROSPECT HOUSE

Meatman is sunning on the balcony
Cutting his toenails in full view
Of mothers and sisters sipping tea
In the garden at half-past three
Of a windy dusty afternoon

As I drive back and forth
In my little tin chugger
I admire his physique
Just look at those fine red shoulders
Suffering in the heat of the day
At night he won't sleep some
Sharptooth fly will have
Dug holes above his knees and I
Will worry his dreams

In The Wilderness

We decided to sleep out on the prairie
zipped naked in one bag
no tent between us and the distant sky

I dreamt we aged quite a bit
our hair grew brittle
our legs got thinner

The wind began to blow

It blew up a gritty storm

We said we ought to get up
and stamp out the fire

The high wind rolled us against a fencepost

A pagewire thorn caught in the skin of my arm

And still we only dreamt the storm and the darkness
nothing could rouse us up out of the grass
until morning when a few flakes of snow
fell on my sleeping hands which were
still gripping the blankets
and the flakes fall and melt on my sleeping hands
each one as it melts staining me
with the tawny stain of speckled age

I cry out in fear
the touch of the snow is like an acid burn
and there you stand in your strength
showing your proud cluster of grey jupiter curls
you dress slowly
you are not even cold in the cold morning
your feet redden in the white grass

I braid my hair

You gently balance a roof of wet twigs
over the ashy fire

About My
WAR

Looking For Uncle Tich in the War Cemetery

o tenderness of heaven rain down on army tombstones this is the song the band plays while under the sun spiders are crawling up hot marble   a time to crawl up a time to swing down again   a time to shrivel leaving the next generation to get to the top and over

a kiosk contains the book which contains the names of the fallen a perfect record of those boxfuls of bones brittle under caved-in coffin lids under stony soil and lilac sky   this is the burrowing beetles' world that the spider knows nothing of

some died with all their flesh on, some with both eyelids to close over both eyes our young guide has the air of a lover on a postcard smarmed-down hair forget-me-not eyes   a bird flies through the picture *is that a hawk* you ask nervously *a falcon* he replies *without master or jess*

when we tell of our uncle here since 1916 not once disturbed by visitors it takes his breath away, *no one here of that name* he sighs and closes the book later we find the little soldier under an alias of his rascally boyhood

tomorrow this place will be closed for the season, shed padlocked, gates barred   the marching band will sit on the grass polishing brass instruments with khaki rags   at a signal each man will get to his feet preparing his lips for the last blow

while the industrious spider lays her eggs in the body of a beetle strayed into the light

Making Up A Four

riding the inevitable train the slow one making
its tedious way across a broken continent

how many hours, how many days of this? I ask the
commandant   look all the refugees
are going the other way.

quiet she says or join in the game
we need a fourth there's nothing else to amuse us
we do have a destination but we're waiting
for our orders on the field telephone

and I know where it is I tell her it's somewhere
unimagined it's where the ashes are stored
it's where the bones are piled up

and when we arrive there'll be one survivor
among the tumbled bricks but still
we'll eat our iron rations   nothing to drink but sweet
army tea dipped from a galvanized pail

it's a lovely day out there, I tell her,
gesturing towards the scorched world
full of stumbling mothers and children
with bundles on their heads
let's stop and get out and have a picnic

irony she says, will get you nowhere
and the three women turn back to their cards
and I to the window where I can see the refugees
grey and literal as a string of donkeys
limping with stones in their hooves

An Offering

there's a farm in god's head
where flocks of creatures dark
and feathery as moths are bred
each tethered to a twig of samphire
or could be a stem of glass
that substance clearly
without crystal

and when they are grown and freed
they fly into our minds
infesting our affections
as the saint proved
I met years ago in Holland
in a hall full of stupified
refugees he was leaning
against the scratched piano
wearing the usual greasy khakis
the usual grimed sneakers
a limp camel lit
between saffron fingers

which lovingly touched
my head scaring up
a cloud of black wings
which I saw then simply
a candid incarnation
of indwelling lice
and from this blessing
from the forgotten smoke
my hair flared and crinkled
charing my scorched brow

now whenever I get close
to the truth this fellow's
weary gesture comes between
me and the holy face
obscuring the light
by which I hope to be blinded
again he breathes into me
that breath of stale teeth
and again the fire leaps
from his hand to my head

the refugee told me his story

they awoke us at night he said
and marched us to the station
where a band was playing
girls held up pitch torches
the flames lighted our faces
but smoke shadows played over our features
so that no one could really be recognized

they told us we were to sing
patriotic songs until the train arrived
of course none of us
could remember the words
LA DEE LA LA *we sang*
DEE DIDDLE DUM DEE
that made them angry
they shouted oaths and began to shoot
no one was hurt, it was too dark to aim
properly   most of us ran
into the forest and escaped
across the border
I never did know said Patrick Valentine
who they were
or where the train would have taken us

SHRAPNEL

shrapnel has torn the man's ribs apart
there is a shabby wound in his breast
his mouth opens innocently upon a cry

he wants to curse his enemies but cannot
for he sees them as striplings lying in the grass
each with a girl beneath him
the long grass full of clover and fieldherbs
waves gently in the heat
the men get up from the women
and buckle on their belts
the women just lie there looking up at the thundery sky
we are wounded with joy they tell each other
we are happy happy happy

the soldier sees this he hears all this
as he lies there asking the earth
is this my final place my own place
he glances upwards to where
the tops of the trees almost meet
there is just a small patch of empty sky showing
it must be spring for a bird with a straw in its beak
swoops down to a low bough   he tries to think
of the name of the bird
he tries to think of his own name
the name of his son who has learned to speak already
so his wife writes   he has seen the child only once
and that was more than a year ago

he tries to remember the colour of his wife's eyes
he sees only her frailty those little narrow birdbones
beneath the soft flesh
he wishes she was another woman
one easier to abandon   one calm and robust
with a wide smooth brow

but who could forget that pitiful teat
in the child's mouth
the curious maze of blue milkveins whose pattern
he traces in the dirt   his hand touches a broken brick
here was a house   now he remembers the collapse
of its walls

he licks his lips tasting for brickdust
he counts his strong teeth with his tongue
they are all there unchipped   he hears the bland
voice of the dentist telling him he has perfect bite

he shuts his eyes against the light but it shines on
through rosy lids which are the same colour exactly
as his wife's secret he wants to part her legs
and touch her glistening vermilion lining
now at last he understands
why he loves the bodies of women
more than the bodies of men   for pale skin covers
a man all over and only a wound can show his lining

carefully he passes his hands over his body
buttoned into its tunic of stiff drab wool
until he finds the hole in his chest
he thrusts in his fist to staunch the blood
a pulse beats close to his folded fingers
it is insistent and strong
it is pushing him away from himself

          in the town square
her hair like a flock
of pigeons flies
up from the clippers
one feathery tuft remains
someone has pinned
a paper to her smock
says something absurd about
fraternizing
who is the enemy?
I ask   she tries to open
eyes swollen to slits
from weeping

just a man she says
and I notice the freckles
on her hands   this is
the first time
I have seen her

she follows me everywhere
to the beer parlour
to the poolhall
but the man's a barber
so we soon get out of there
to Tilly's where one of the girls
tries to lend her a hat
she follows as though
we were fastened together
with a rope

a passer-by remarks
that the rope is invisible
I am surprised
it feels heavy enough

and when I look down
there it is
yellow as plaited tow

she follows me to the end of town
past ducks swimming on an oily
dugout   to the dump
and there is her hair
dark fronds and single strands
strewn about on soapflakes boxes
and over some sodden plates
and cups of copper-coloured paper

       when we come to a grimy hut
naturally we go in together
but she stands so long
staring through the cloudy
pane of window
that the set of her features
becomes blurred in my mind

at last she turns
and lays her cold self down
on the broken cot
fear-streamers ray from her head

and a mouth opens
it is a small dark hole
her face is greyer
than the pillow

WHAT A GIRL HAS

When he was a young man
in the German war
my cousin learned a lot
of barrack-room songs

now that he's getting on
he still sings them on Sundays
to the tune of a breathy concertina

> *"If I had what a girl has*
> *If I had what a girl has*
> *I would lie all day at the crossroads*
> *With my legs spread apart"*

No you wouldn't Leon
if you were a girl
you wouldn't do it like that

you would sit in an oaktree
playing softly on your mandolin
with seven colors of ribbon
tied to its stem

you would sit on a branch
and let your bare feet hang down
over the swaying heads
of the endless marching columns
going towards the battlefront
if some of those soldiers
didn't hear your song
did not look up and grasp your dangling feet
and pull you down from the tree
and rape you in the rising dust

then that would be their loss
wouldn't it cousin?

SITTING UNDER DEATH'S RICH SHADE

in June I visited a charnel house
in Holland I was searching
for a friend   I wore black gloves
the attendant showed me great respect

it is tidy in there
smells faintly of the dark earth
at Easter the members of the Sepulchre Society
polish up the bones and arrange
them in order of rank and sanctity

I was looking for a huge bony skull
with a small round hole
in the left temple
—a healer had once trephined the head
to let out evil—

when I had found him
I knotted him into my kerchief
and carried him home

Frans I began
I have so much to tell you
will you or won't you hear
my confession?

he was silent   smiled sadly

Frans I told him
may I say at last
that once I desired you? a bit
of me is broken
because of your memory

no tears fall from dead eyes
his grin becomes toothy, lascivious

damn you I cry out
you would not take me
when I was fifteen and dangerous

BURNING THE STUBBLE

travelling toward the city at night
we remark five brilliant fires
burning in the west suburbs

it's like when we were children in the country
watching mounds of raked straw
burning in the fields

these were garrisons of defenders
our driver explains in a low voice
trapped in the collapse of their barracks

no one invaded   the attack came from within
after a week the stench became unbearable
there were whispers of plague in the street
rumours of cholera   *the citizens poured on gasoline*
set a torch to it all

by the time we arrive the women are already at work
pulling hot skeletons from the ashes
each imagines she can recognize
her particular family
the husband, the young sons, a bachelor uncle
a stranger taken in

the remains are stacked up in irregular piles
then all of us take a hand
shovelling on rubble and dirt
dirt and rubble

the winter is long and dark
there are heavy falls of snow
ice moves down from the north
the mounds become a range
of low white drumlins

by spring not one of us remembers
that the foundation of every hill
is a heap of charred fragments

About My War

you, stranger at my table, ask
what did you do when you were young?
I don't answer at once
am stirring something
in a great iron pot

I was a soldier
I reply at last
we were a band of partisans
fighting in the green mountains

I can see that you don't really believe me
your eyes are on my breasts
(yes they are massive
overshadowing the soup)
I was dropped behind the lines
I explain desperately
bringing explosives
and a shortwave radio

you fall silent, disappointed
that I was not a dancer
entertaining the troops
(we huge women were all once beautiful)

you watch my hands tearing a salad of green leaves
I take a cloth, wipe a spatter of gravy from my arm
and all this time I have been staring
through the water-sheeted window
it has rained for three days
blue shallows lie
on the sodden grass

then the door slams open
and in comes the master from the storm
he does not greet us
throws down his wet cape
it glistens on the floor

see that no one walks on my lawn
he says   *the tread of boots*
could churn it to a field of mud

she's arranging irises in a polished brass vase as elegant and nar-row-shouldered as herself   *made from a bombcase* she explains to the tall blue flags stiff as april that will not obey her arthritic fingers *1916* she adds softening the effect with a spray of ferny leaves

bombs falling on london all around the town whistling down from silvery zeppelins which nose about in the sky huge docile fish swimming in the upper air

she stalks naked through the dark rooms watching her reflection flicker in grey mirrors   soft thin body, pale legs, wiry red hair resting uneasily on white shoulders and freckled arms   she peers closer examines the small uneven face the emphatic mouth the smallpox scar between the foxy brows

this is the first time she has ever been alone in the forest-hill house where she was born

if ever she was born for there's no record of any such birth of any such person as herself, none   she found that out at her wedding five months ago *you are marrying nobody* and she rests her fingers lightly on the two stars on william's epaulette then leans forward and kisses him on the mouth she can feel that her warm lips shock him for he's younger and much shyer than she is   *bill my will* she whispers again to the dark house this lone-ly night *can you survive all this?   can I?*

for she carries in her velvet belly a weight lighter than a burr a kernel from which a red-haired child may grow

now she's in the cool garden hugging her thin arms round her fine nakedness chalkwhite roses bloom in their beds their stems and thorns black as blood   one open flower stares up at her with the pinched face of an infant about to cry the earth shrieks   cracks apart   rumbles   shakes shakes   and trembles to a stop

fish has laid his tumble of eggs among the pavements and the houses   the school crumples   the churchtower falls into the park   the walls of the prison break open and men rush out thanking the fishgod for their deliverance almost at once they turn into muddy soldiers grumbling and joking about the war, the mud, wet feet, rats and the rotten bitter war

she lies flat in the roses covered with plaster dust from next door thorns clawing at her chin and her breasts the cocklebur little nut moves within her parts from its seedcase and drops from her to the earth followed by a narrow warm trickle

she scratches among the roses as a cat might then buries the tiny thing, without a tear stands up dizzy lighter by the weight of a handful of leaves

in the house she draws the heavy curtain so close that not a chink parts them then lights a candle and flings herself onto the wide bed   a small empty space aches within her, aches coldly through her sleep which lasts long into the next day

downstairs in the back kitchen where the window is broken and the door swings loose on its hinges the small debris of the city has been sifting into the house all night a layer of fine particles covers the sink and the green glass flower-holders   by morning the shelf and the vases that stand there—blue raku, enamelled chinoiserie, silver beaten thin as steam—are greyed with a layer of fine detritus which might be the dust of a century almost asleep charles hears his mother say to her friend I don't care what you're wearing I don't care what you've been eating just come over here and sit down beside me at the piano   in bed the child is telling himself the story of everything that has happened   the man sitting beside his mother playing and singing *to althea from prison* which the boy interprets as the tale of the heart's refusal he falls into a dream of wisteria a bower outside a tavern in italy where anything grows claims his mother but here in this beastly climate it's hard to find a flowering creeper though there are climbing shrubs enough to cover any balcony with a thicket of tender leaves where linnets nest and sing

the boy sees himself in the attic fondling the trailing teagown his aunt is said to have put away forever when word came that her lover had been picked off by a sniper charles lifts it out of its squashed cardboard box and slips it over his head the chiffon is a turbid green like ditchwater for a moment the gown hangs silkily on his naked shoulders then with a whisper falls apart and floats to the floor each piece no bigger than an envelope he gathers them all up and folds them back into the blue tissue assuring himself that after a year the garment will heal and become whole and beautiful again he has only to be patient and wait the twelvemonth through

from downstairs the sound of the two voices the four hands trails away to silence the child makes himself think of those twenty fingers resting on the piano keys he would like to be another person a boy his own age but with different coloured eyes and hair lying on the bottom of the sea looking up through grey water at the metal hull of a ship passing overhead   in the first class ballroom two golden-haired women have just finished playing a duet on the piano the last trickle of sound dribbles out into the ocean   the strange boy puts out a languid hand and catches the music in the guise of undulating seaweed *charles darling* his mother has said it more than once your uncle norman is the owner of an excellent baritone when she says *charles darling* he's always startled because that's how she speaks to his father the first charles who perhaps has returned and is standing behind him in his majesty's uniform the tropical one because he's just arrived from a redhot place where mangos grow on a tall tree a man in a turban shakes the tree and when the fruit falls he makes it into chutney which the officers eat from dishes like pink porcelain blossoms while the brown soldiers sit on blankets spread over the dead grass and are served nothing but hard round cakes of rivermud arranged in neat rows on old tin trays rusting a little at the rims

it's afternoon and nurse is pinning a terry square on one of the twins who are the result she says candidly of his father's last leave or maybe that mr norman but no she laughs darkly he'd rather be godfather to many than father to one   he's not such a bad sort for doesn't he take the twins off our hands most afternoons and give us all a rest from their squalling

the man whom the boy hates picks up the babies one under each arm and dumps them into the perambulator   as he starts off it begins to rain pittering on the pramhoods but that doesn't bother uncle who strides away up the village singing his loudest   nurse and charles watch him go until they can't hear the singing and crying any more then she goes upstairs to tidy and he picks up the book he's decided to read about fighter aircraft not that he cares much for it but it makes him feel more like some of the boys he goes to school with

norman is back the babies are asleep in their soft white shawls smelling of their mother's sandlewood soap she's in a silly mood and comes giggling out of the drawing room inviting the man to stay as though he was a stranger she was meeting for the first time it's tea and cake in the summerhouse   charles is not included he has his in the kitchen with nurse when he turns his head and looks through the kitchen window he can see the creepers growing up the side of the summerhouse where rain is still dripping from the eaves a large drop is hanging from the lip of one of the greenish cobea blossoms he can't make up his mind whether it will trickle down the striped purple throat of the flower or whether it will fall outwards onto the leaves which are withering and turning pink with autumn

a storm comes at night and charles gets up trembling wanting to creep into bed with nurse who is not afraid of anything he knows her back turned towards him in sleep will smell reassuringly of buttered bread   on the turn of the stair he sees his mother with uncle norman their hands are clasped tightly but she is holding the man away from her by the length of her white freckled arms   thunder breaks the air then hush a very faint word comes from between her lips what's she saying what's she saying?

the next streak of lightning lifts her hair which stands up all around her head like a brilliant foxfur halo   little white tongues of flame flash from the curled ends of her red hair

uncle norman whimpers and lets go and she sinks down onto the stairs moaning or crying or laughing it's difficult to tell which   charles decides she is laughing and goes back to bed to dream of italy where the three of them stayed in a room above a courtyard *so long* father says buckling on his sam browne looking into his son's eyes for a long time

then he picks up his cap and swaggerstick from the chair by the brass bed where his wife is lying with the quilt pulled up over her face refusing to look refusing to say goodbye

She IMPORTUNES
GOD

Woman Reading In Bath

I am swimming alone on the dark sea
When before me looms up the great stout chin of god
Floating on the black chops of the high tide
And his hands are clutching the slippery wet sides
The edges and the hems of his bungled universe

What's this curling murderously around my neck?
What's this strangling over the blue knots of my neck?
Wiry fingers of hair thick knuckle-bladders
It is a long curled lock from the godhead
Red as sargassum

When the eye is shut then shall the great globe dim
Like a popped bulb scattering flakes
Of slowly falling volcano glass round
The vast bulges of softly swimming belly
And does the great thumping creator's heart
Somehow sit inside and direct the traffic
Of sharks and seals and obedient shoals?
Lucky and cunning from the dark I watch
The huge mouthful of deified teeth from which
Squeaks out a puny cry meant to be a roar
Great heave of the chest but yet a breath
So small it hardly blows my hair about
As I tread water in the shallows
Under the square shadow of his shoulders
        He heaves up on stick legs like a fat bird
 Crack crack the shanks have snapped
And down he flops on the shingles gasping and stranded

I—the Director—pick up the phone
Connecting me to the sky and the undersea silt
I say *"Birds come down from the clouds"*

I say *"Great crabs come up from the deep*
Chew on this mass—feed all your children
On it for a year"

Oh what a dry and brittle skeleton he makes
But on the last day a small bone hand shall creep
Out of the gray shore sand
And grasping a pebble throw it over my head
Into deep water

Jesus was given a bride Alice Long
her flowering skirt
touched the toes of her shoes,
the marriage took place
at the City Conservatory

the high glass roof
was out of the range of her eyes
when she looked up at the green canopy
the tops of the trees were tossing about
in a fierce wind
but among the pots of coleus
and chrysanthemums
on the forest floor
there was not a sound nor a breeze

there she lay down faithfully
and her damp bed was mossy
she said: *my desire is a wood strawberry*
              I have hung it in my breast
              on a string of twisted hair

in the morning when she awakened
God had become a baby with a wizened face
before noon she had taught him to speak

              we are not alone
              we are not alone
              we are not alone
              Alice he said
              we are not

On the first morning, we saw a road stretching before us, and this road was one long word reaching from here to there. How enticingly clear and simple this seemed. At once, we packed bread and cheese and knives and skins of fresh water and set out with a will upon our journey.

At the close of that day, the road and the word came to an end, and we struck camp for the night. On the second day there was another road, another word. And so it went on. However, at the end of the sixth day things were a little different. Because we had stopped on our way to pick the serviceberries that grew by the side of the road, we arrived late at our camping place. It was already dusk, and we were so tired that we threw ourselves down on the grassy verge without as much as taking off our boots or washing our faces. Indeed, we were so tired that we even forgot our evening prayer to our creator, the Demiurge Y, he who had undoubtedly arranged this journey for us and watched over us as we travelled.

When we awoke, the midmorning sun was hot upon our upturned faces. Above us, in the blue dome of the sky there was not a single cloud, simply a sentence made up of all the words from the past week. The message was simple and direct. As soon as we read it, we fell into momentary despair, for, up to then, we had thought ourselves innocent, or almost so. Truly, we were not deserving of such a judgement.

There was no road and no direction. Would there ever be again? Here we were in the wilderness with no one to guide us. Though our hearts beseeched the Demiurge, he did not heed us. Well, there was nothing for it but to make the best of things, and so we lazed through the day in the long fragrant grass. Even the insects joined us in our rest, and nipped at our skin so gently that we hardly noticed their bites.

Of course Y did not allow us more than one day of rest. The next morning we were off again pursuing the word and the truth with a little less enthusiasm than before, yet still curious to know where the road would eventually lead us.

Now the pattern was set, and we continued for what seemed like centuries in the same way. On every seventh day the week's words were added to those already crowding the sky, and every sentence was more difficult and threatening than the last one. It was not surprising that the Demiurge had decreed a sabbath of rest. We could imagine that it could take him a whole day to compose a suitably abusive judgement for the next week's journey.

As for us mortals, we were glad to stop on the road to fill our flasks with fresh spring water and to enjoy the scenery and the warm sunny weather. When cool evening fell, we began our sabbath dance, watching the shadows of our gestures move gracefully under the moon.

Y was obviously not at all pleased with our lightheartedness, for his words became every week more forbidding and his path more rigorous. In some places it was overgrown with thorny weeds, and in others it was ankle deep in stinking brackish water. Our creator had made up his mind that we were to travel among the sharp stones, grasping at stinging nettles, and even at poison ivy if we were so foolish as not to recognize its trinity.

One Wednesday morning, as we were wandering along a flinty road that passed through a rock strewn valley, the enamel sky, which must have become overburdened with the many curses and judgements written upon it, cracked and split into a thousand, thousand pieces. One moment the sky was full of words, the next flakes of blue were falling upon the earth like scurf from the unwashed heads of angels.

And these flakes floated down upon the grass and the stones and the hills and the rivers and the bitter oceans. They alighted too on all the birds and the beasts, even upon our friends the insects. And from this falling all creation received its voice. Never was there such a roaring and a twittering and a buzzing and a squealing. As for us poor wanderers, we too received this blessing. Our ears and our mouths were opened, and we shouted and sang and argued until our throats were sore.

Now there could be no more sky words, and no more need for us to travel the earth. This was the place of our deliverance. We made up our minds to settle in this spot and to build a city with the stones that lay around us. Here we live still, passing the days in discussions and quarrels and the evenings in the singing of bawdy ballads and the telling of tall tales.

No longer are we confined to gesture and the written word. Indeed we have almost forgotten how to read and write so happy are we with the speeches and lies which come effortlessly to our tongues.

As for our master the Demiurge, he has been defeated by his own cruelty and arrogance, for he among all beings did not receive a voice. The sky of words fell downward only, and Y was far too proud to descend from his heaven and accept the gift of speech. In his high place he is silent still, though every now and then he throws down his orders and curses in a written scroll or codex. Of course, we never read these for we are far too busy chatting and boasting and reciting for that.

However, we are not entirely lacking in piety. In the very centre of our city we have built a modest temple to contain these holy objects. Sometimes one of our children, with the natural curiosity of the young, demands to learn to read and to discover the secrets locked up in those pages. Then we gently explain that our revered creator, Yaldabaoth the Demiurge, has promised to punish with terrible severity the impious fool who dares disturb the dusty silence that lies forever upon his words.

GERALD

The spiritual advisor, he told us to call him Gerald, commanded us all to kneel. Most did so, but a few of us held out against a demand we felt to be humiliating. Then we were to put our hands on our heads as a token of submission. None of us did that. After all why should we debase ourselves simply to please a power-hungry old man?

We were surprised when we heard his ancient cackle of a laugh, astonished when he praised the rebellious ones. "Obedience can be a sin," he explained, "in certain circumstances." We imagined a circle within which the more timid of us were trapped, but others ran boldly about and were not confined by any particular system of thought.

It took us only a day to realize that in fact we had all been bamboozled, for if we were disobedient again then it could be concluded that we were confined by our need for praise, our slavish desire to please the hierophant. That's how we regarded him now, simply as an old teacher of orthodoxies, with all sorts of tricks up his sleeve to catch out any of us who leaned dangerously towards independent ideas.

Nothing, we knew, had changed since our world began, this small world of our studies, our constant striving towards the light. The path is dusty and the road is thorny. We knew that of course, and we accepted as inevitable the sharp stones of Gerald's disapproval as we became a group united against the holy old reprobate.

He would try to conquer us; we would resist him. We held secret meetings to discuss all sorts of ways of cheating him. Maddingly he appeared to take no notice, "All these little venial sins are of no importance," he seemed to be telling us. Indeed he forgave us everything. He beamed indulgently upon us. Can you imagine how infuriating this was? After all, we had not come here to be pandered to, like a bunch of silly children.

It was then that we decided to separate. Perhaps we had misunderstood the dictum, *divide and conquer.* Each of us took a different road to the destruction of the old man's argument. We forgot the words, *united front, common purpose,* all that sort of rubbish. We were no longer a pack of wild dogs nipping at his ideas. Each of us became his own creature. We even went so far as to wear badges to denote our differences: a tiger, an anaconda, a scorpion, a fierce but elegant rogue elephant. This last was of course myself. I felt huge wearing that badge. But I knew as did the others, that we were now not just contending against our sainted master, but against one another. We were each as likely to injure another student as we were to hurt His Reverence. Could a tiger, I constantly asked myself, leap upon the back of an elephant and sever its spine with one bite? If I, the elephant, were to step upon the scorpion would her sting prove mortal to me, as my tread would certainly be to the venomous little arachnid?

Thus had the sly old master divided his enemies. Now he could conquer us one by one. We would not even want to call upon each other for help. Nothing could save us from the cage, the circle, the swap and the sellout.

And so he has won our souls, and we are obedient to him, though not slavishly so. For Gerald has left this world and left it to us, his students. As we watch an old woman grinding his bones on the mountainside, we are brought to the realisation that his dust and the taste of it pervades all of us. We eat him, we breathe him, we take up into our own bones the Geraldessence which will certainly divide us and pollute us, as much as it will bring us together and make us one.

the compassion of the one whose residence is a speck of dust a
grain of sand or salt the bubble of spit on the lip of the dying
the one who has led us to believe that the word is short almost
square it might be *come* or *go* or *desire* but nothing longer than
that

a drop of rain falls into the ocean and we are commanded to
recognize this one globule as separate from all the rest by its
freshness perhaps or by its shape which like the planet's is spher-
ical but imperfectly so

air surrounds us then the canopy of ozone which angels pierce
as they ascend from the tangent plane at any of the possible
angles   how hard it is to see them as they dart through the tun-
nel of our sight

harder still to perceive their descent their legs slightly parted the
ball of each pale foot poised over that house of many rooms
whose windows look out on every acre of dirt whether it is
desert or forest or a place we have laid out for ourselves a gar-
den full of birds and worms and creeping plants which
promised on their seed packets to flower, we believed them and
have been disappointed   yet by faith we see buds as the angels
who are god's pupils see us

The Holy Fountain

seeing virgins walk
along the banks of a river
who can believe that they will one day be sore?
walking on thin straight legs
bunched together or in single file
wobbling along a sea wall or standing
still on separate posts of a breakwater
as they watch the sea go out
across the empty sound

who can believe that
they will one day be sore?
or slowly plod
heavy with full-term child?

will they arch with desire
and cannot come?

who can believe that at this time of year
seeing men standing
in pissing attitudes
in corners of buildings or by trees
or in the open where the arc is widest
who can believe
that they are so easily buttoned?

did you know that there is an old woman
dressed all in black whose
business it is to defile the altar of Saint Paul?
she is singing about the spider
she is cursing the spider
she is the terrible spider
turning turning and wetting down her legs

now that the well
is boarded up because of the smell
she is the only one who celebrates
the fate of virgins

THE MAN FROM TOLEDO

The man from Toledo used to sit
every evening drinking
from an ugly square cup

his hands have always been much
older than the rest of him
thick veins stand out on them
a system of blue tunnels
only half submerged
in the papery surface
they used to rest so quietly
one turned upward on his knee
the other bent around
the thick angle of his glass

Did you know that he was once
the boss of an african project?
standing with his hat on his head
and a blueprint clutched
in his hand like a whip
his feet were always placed firmly
a little apart and neither itched
nor moved when the drums beat
only his eyes followed the dark legs
of satiny ladies
as they walked by his window
in the warm dusk

One cold morning
in a white saskatchewan spring
a fiery tongue rested
for a moment on his head
his wife was pleased regarding it
as some sort of happy omen easter hat

the man from Toledo felt the weight of virtue
strutted in his sunday suit and gave
five-minute exhibitions of
speaking in tongues

he insisted on a ministry of healing
there are so many lovely women
suffer from acne and sagging breasts
from fat legs and bloodless lips
his love flowed over milky from the cup
and he decided to lay his hands
on every one of them

last sunday evening when
the meeting was hushed and thinking of food
and listening to the sound of its own breathing
he suddenly leapt up screaming and dancing and singing
he saw her at last huge figure of Mother Africa
and with her key-white teeth
she bit through his parted lips

a fire was in him
it licked the dome of his satisfaction
it ran in all his arteries
a string of athletes were his corpuscles
his tears dried in the sparkle of his upward gaze

an odour of juices rose up
from her thighs and her grapefruit breasts
swung free out of her cloth
and trapped him into her flesh

he melted into her and became
the skin of her stinging palms
as she clapped and clapped them together

high above Granny's head
stars are staring and burning
in the slate-blue deep
Granny ties her shawl tighter
around her white ears
and shuts her eyes
and takes off for the great indoors

into the stuffy kitchen
into the tidy house
where everything's strictly folded
everything carefully dusted
(in case she may one day be found dead
she won't leave disorder behind her
for neighbours to tidy up after she's gone)

here Granny sits in her comfortable swivel rocker
licking a dripping Fudgsicle
staring at a sparkling coloured
important message from CTV
three young men and a girl
all very lively and hairy are yelling
and twanging against a background
of swaying plastic ribbons and tinsel tassels

Granny looks and licks contentedly
while the tickless clock on the table
soundlessly marks the division of
evening from night   and Timothy
the cat watches the drips on the floor
drip drip from Granny's sweet treat
Timothy watches as though the drips
were drops of blood from a rat
he had killed and was too fastidious to eat

Suddenly a voice out of heaven: *"Turn off the TV Granny*
Put on your second-best
fur coat
Put out the cat"

saith the Lord

"Walk in the yard Granny
Look up at the stars
Give me your honest opinion
of my handiwork"

saith the Lord

"Why are you piercing holes in me
you wretched nightlights far away"

said Granny lying back in the snow
with her long feet pointing upward
now I know creation is a half-hour drama
I'm watching endlessly
it's a soap opera which never dies
and will always deliver
a daily installment forever and ever

but she stretched her knotty fingers out
far into darkness until they almost touched
the light bursting from the expanding galaxies

"Damn you God" said the old lady
breathing her last in the frozen potato patch

"All I asked was a Kozy Korner
kitchen cushion cat
chum chew chat
spit spite spat

tell telephone TV
chitter chatter chide
snit snigger snide

What do you mean?
grow groan grain?
green gold grey?
bow be burdened bear?

You have known all along that I don't care
for the fundamental   that I live for the incidental
O Lord stop bugging me do
who am I to call my children's children
out of the plastic playbox
out of charm school
to prance among the stars?"

like the ascending Christ
Granny left her print upon the Earth
not a foot only but broad beam
bowed shoulders and corrugated coiffe
as she fell from the rolling planet
as her small innocent self dived and cavorted
among the heavenly bodies
"Amen" sang the angels

"Amen" said Tim the cat
as he jumped through the bathroom window
and silently sat in her chair

WISE QUEENIE, WISE QUEEN

Pig poems abound, but Queenie is matchless,
her heartfelt desire for Jack Pig,

her nose in a bucket of swill,
her freedom to root among the tiny potatoes.

Sui, Sui, my love, my love—
that's how I call her to me.

Five piglets, four and a runt,
which she wisely eats.

Next time, she sighs under her warm pigbreath,
all will be voted in—like a parliament.

No, more like a committee of equals. God
if you want to call it that.

Passover

This is the burden of the solitary prisoner, eating alone like a dog at his dish. And, for lack of a companion, he is eating himself. For every man needs to share his grey hunk of bread. There he sits getting neither fatter nor thinner, and it's always Friday Dinner with no candles to light. It's always an evening in June, drawing in so very slowly towards dark.

Outside a dog is chained to the shadow of his kennel. A woman bends before him, offering an enamel plate of scraps. The dog cannot hide his disappointment; he has waited so many years for an invitation to supper. Every night he wonders, will this be the day of deliverance, when I'll sit up at the table with my paws on the white cloth, waiting for my portion, waiting for Father to fill my cup with milk.

For surely by now they have forgiven my attack on the baby, how I leapt upon her snarling and worrying. That was long ago, but still this tether is a chain of events, one leading inevitably to another, and yet one more.

But then, is it possible for a prisoner to turn his crime into triumph? Is it possible for a dog to cease longing to be a man?

GREEN

A woman longs to make her home in the green of a candle flame. How to do this? First she takes a taper and lights it at the fire. The fire lies in her mind like a dog waiting to bite. The dog lies across the threshhold of the house she wants to enter.

After lighting the candle, she importunes God about her dilemma. *Though I bash on the door with my fist, though I step over his dangerous head, grant that this dog does not waken, that his teeth do not tear at me. However, if he should indeed bite, put it into his head to stop and lick up my blood from the doorstep, so that I have time to limp into the house, that house painted the same green as the inside of this candle flame.*

The woman knows very well that this is the sort of prayer God hears over and over, more than a thousand times every hour, but doesn't that simply mean that she is one human in a vast field of humankind, one flame amongst all the other flames of supplication? In each flame there is the red of anguish, there is the hot white of desire, but there is not always that small curve of green, for if it were so every candlestand would appear from a distance like a pointed hill of growing grass sprinkled with flowers of light.

That would not do at all, for then the woman would have no choice to make. Greenness would be all around. She would have to dwell in it willy-nilly her whole life through: in the meadows, in the forest, in the sea. Perhaps she would forever view the world through the green eyes of a certain species of seal. She might even be forced to find her home in a piece of seatossed bottle glass thrown up upon the shore.

But her fears are groundless. At her knock the door opens quickly, and she jumps over the dog who makes a fruitless snap towards her crotch. He tries a second time, but she's through already and sitting on a long pale sofa patterned with waterlily leaves. God is at the hearth lighting a fire of green boughs. Presently he sits down beside her. *Well now my dear,* he murmurs, leaning caringly towards her. *Shall it be mint tea, or absinthe perhaps, in a viridian cup?*

A Girl Dreams

of a sleeping man

she leans forward as though over the open roof of her dollhouse and watches the man's dream

the girl is lying in her bed in the nursery on the top floor of a house more than two hundred years old   within her lies the man she has dreamed up   he is careful not to disturb her   he breathes to the very same rhythm she does turns when she turns tries to synchronize his heartbeat with hers   their double breath is exhaled through the child's nostrils and ascends to the ceiling where a ring of painted plaster cherubs prances around a frosted glass lamp   the breath of generations of children has smeared the cherub's colours   they have become grey and chalky

the girl is fast asleep but she has the sensation of opening her eyes and noticing the five little fellows with their ribbons and their garlands   then her sight turns inward once more and she concentrates on the man who is dreaming of a dog with a human head   presently that changes and he becomes a human boy with the head of a dog

the dogboy is foolish enough to be happy about his new form indeed he is quite smug about it   this annoys the girl and she wants to interfere at once and change the dogperson into some-one more curious afraid and disenchanted

she asks herself does this creature yap or does he speak? in his mind does he lie pampered and useless in a padded dogbasket? or does he think of himself as a dangerous huskie sleeping out in the winter night under a quilt of snow?

she makes up her mind that he's far too tame for that much tamer in fact than any ordinary boy   he shall lie in a wooden bed with muslin sheets much like the one in her dollhouse though bigger of course but is it right for her to make these decisions for him   after all he is not in her dream he belongs to the man   it's true that she has dreamed the man but how far can she go   does a man in a dream have free will can he have independent dreams or do they in some way belong to her.

the girl thinks about this for some time   *your imagination is your own* she tells the man at last but don't forget that you are bound to let me know all your dreams and conjectures   the rule is that I can see everything but I am not allowed to change it   this seems fair and the man agrees

later they begin to quarrel about whether the people in the man's dream are to be told that the girl is watching them and no doubt making her own judgments of their shapes and their deeds   *it will make them happy* the girl argues to know that I am interested in them that from a distance I wish them well   that perhaps I even love them in my own detached way

no says the man firmly they are never to hear of your existence for they would be unable to accept your curiosity   any more than you dearest child can accept the fact that one of those grubby little angels up there—I shall not tell you which—is watching and judging you   that with his faded blue eye he is following your every move

Death &
OTHER
ABSTRACTIONS

evening, she says, is very like morning
when the sky is streaked and one pointed star
dangles on a fine string in the window

of understanding   the question
is very clear, but the answer is blurred as though
too many mouths were singing different words
to the same tune

no one can say how many keys
there are to the lock
of music and cutting more
can do no good

let swatches of hair white and gold
fall where they may

and now, she says, I'll lie down
on my bed of prevarications
while the sun apparently gets up, goes down
according to the whim of my lover

you've met him, the one
playing stars and stripes
snakes and ladders
against the twilight sky

obscuring my vision
of angels turning eastward
chanting their creed
affirming their belief in light
and of course in darkness

which after all is nothing
more than the earth mooning
her backside to the sun

BIGOS

Speculation comes easily to the man who can't tell the difference between this and that reality. His habit is to accept or reject each day, as though it was nothing more than a scrap of roasted lamb, offered at arm's length, on the point of a knife.

Often he dreams of severed limbs, but is never quite sure whose arms and thighs these once were. He has decided it doesn't matter. He likes them like that, unattached, flung far from what lies at the centre. Far from this head, whose mouth speaks endlessly, as though it might be a sin to leave a breath's pause on the tape.

It's only when he's gone, the one distance, the one direction possible, that we can bring ourselves to play the whole thing back. And then, of course, he seems to speak to us out of another time. But is there more than one?

That was always his question, and now that he's out there, it's natural we should think of him carefully gathering up the dust of his bones, for every atom of this white grit must be fitted together before he can begin on the flesh, his answer.

His wife dries her tears on a napkin of leaves, and lies with his brother under the open sky, calculating the propinquities of genes. For her there is no extension or bending of the light. Her desire is to get on with this life. But first she must find, in the depths of heaven, his one clear abiding star.

So perfect is her longing, that she has forgotten the iron pot, left balanced over the campfire. By now the hunter's stew has burned to the metal.

All night the lovers scrape and scour. Will they never be able to divide one substance from another?

The Restoration

the house, the first in the district
built of fieldstones, still stands
on the lush flats in the shadow
of round dry hills, all this
mind you in a valley far lower
than the prairie   it's where
in archeotime the sea was
that covered our beginnings
those layers of ammonites
worms and sea cucumbers
that prefigure us

the fieldstone house by the blind
lake where uncle drowned himself
in nineteen-twenty-eight
aunt visits there on anniversaries
of the tragedy, flies in
at great expense from elegant toronto

as soon as she's seated in that particular
rocker in that particular room
uncle appears looking handsome and sly
as the day he dove in, sits in his old
armchair, crosses his legs, scrabbles
in his pocket for a sweet marie
peels off the wrapper, lets it fall
on the livingroom carpet
never so much as looks
at the old woman, never offers
her a bite, when he's finished
just fades out like a line of bushes
in the dusk   leaves her to pick
up after him, which she does
grumbling at the lakewater
slopped everywhere
at the bluegreen algae clinging
to his wet footprints

night cries which once were owls in the woodlot
have become the calls of an ambulance
tearing through the streets to the morgue

what's the hurry asks the corpse in a gentle voice

the driver-paramedic doesn't have an answer
he keeps his eyes on the traffic
his thoughts on a kind woman
he has known since childhood
her hand on his shoulder his head on her breast

he's uneasy for lately she seems to be turning away
in the dark from his melancholy
his not caring any longer
whether he's doing the exact right thing
according to the rules
which tell him how the face of a corpse
should be covered

seeds of light are falling like tears on the verges
of the streets through which he is hurrying
they germinate in the pavement spring up
with coloured branches with brilliant flowers
meanwhile a figure known as cruel frost lies supine
on every roof ordering the snow and icicles
demanding that the smoke rise
straight up from the chimney

the dead person sees and understands
but cannot move a finger
shut my eyes she begs

the man stops suddenly in the middle of an intersection
he's wearing a white coat and regulation cap
which he tips with his index finger
signifying his respect for the dead

he has remembered that the manual says
to check females for pregnancy
oh her belly is a hard and squirming dome
god give me a knife he prays
that I may bring forth this child
slippery and bloody yet alive

and he wonders could it have been his own
in some other place full of rural temptations
where a log hut backs on the forest
the one window looking over a small barnyard
and beyond that a couple of ploughed fields
there on winter nights the boreal owl
hunts mice in the furrows

albert is haranguing his mother about his name complaining as
usual about how unsuitable it is she knows that then why for
godsake? she tells how once there was a royal prince but when
he came to be king he was suddenly george like the rest

you don't know how embarrassing it is in class among the marks
and olivers even james is a king and a saint   at our school saint
simeon stylites has it over all the rest *saint simeon's secondary
school* he yells these words at her over and over this argument is
finished call yourself al or bertie or whatever you want I'm
going in to take a bath and she drops her trowel and coarse
leather gloves into the low basket she's using for weeds

albert is into wild plants and doesn't call anything a weed it is
his belief that darnel and alexanders will inherit the earth from
his mother's damask roses which have been tame since the time
of the persians xerxes would have been a fair name or xenophon
good thing I'm not a girl she might have named me rose tokio
rose I love you I'll always dream of you some of those japanese
cultivars have poison hips pip hooray but then consider *rosa
centifolia muscosa* its crowded petals and many weak thorns even
the buds are edible

at the funeral he insists they are to call him mr carew now that
he's head of the family what family counters the reverend you
are the last of the bunch albert and anyway you are fifteen and
a ward of the court my mother spoke of a half-sister replies mr
carew with dignity he is led to an overgrown part of the church-
yard here lies rozalia daughter of euphemia you women he
accuses them in his heart have gone before me and left me alone
in this social blaze while you rest in your cool tombs

PARADIJSLAAN

A month's holiday can so easily become a sojourn of years. Stay for awhile and you'll find yourself a citizen of a foreign country, all this in the blink of a farsighted eye. Soon you'll be walking a dog along streets with names in a language which isn't even written in the alphabet you grew up with. Blah. Blah, blah— you're speaking in a twisted tongue you hadn't even heard before you were thirty. You're letting the dog off the leash to run in a park where the grass is a paler green than you ever dreamed of. You're throwing him sticks, you're calling his name, whatever that is. Even your whistling is in a peculiar key you once heard on the radio in a programme devoted to oriental music. Is that it? Have you gone East—or South perhaps? Is it natural after all for every bush to blossom with scarlet flowers as big as teacups?

On the way back to your apartment you catch sight of a street you never noticed before. And when you turn down it you are passing plane trees and modest houses built of brick, a substance you haven't seen for years. Aha, you say, I am on my way, and you quicken your walk until it becomes a dance. The dog has left you, of course. You toss away the pointless empty leash.

You are almost there. You are almost home. Number eighteen, number twenty, number twenty-two, the old place. When you knock will anyone open the door? When you press the bell will it echo in the hallway past the hatrack with its five polished brass hooks, past the umbrella stand made from an elephant's forefoot?

It's up to you to decide why you have come back, Aunt says, twisting a grey curl round the second finger of her left hand.

But you know why you've come. Dying is an old-fashioned thing to do and it's best done in the same house where all this began.

No need to hurry. It'll take you a few months you reckon, maybe even a year or two. You will recline on the worn leather sofa. Staring through the window whose wavering glass is like water, you will watch the seasons change the garden. There, pinned to the fence, are the trees you remember as saplings. At times they are bare, at times full of blossom, at times heavy with fruit. And you'll understand at last what Jesus meant when he said to the apostles, *Today I have planted three trees for you in Paradise.*

The tears I shed, *she tells me,* more than filled my bathtub. They splashed over the edges and soaked into the rugs and the curtains. They seeped through the walls and dripped through the floor. When I rolled back the carpet there was a damp white deposit, thick enough to be scratched with a thumbnail, coating the pine planks. Then, just as I feared, some officious person flung open the windows and let in all the sharp air of autumn. I was left staring at a stained floor and a salt-encrusted tub. Later I noticed that a few driblets had escaped the airing by hiding behind the joists. These dropped, an unnatural dew, upon the room below. There was not enough though to cause more than a few spots on the furniture and a persistent, though not unpleasant, briny smell. *And she stares down at her crooked feet grimed black from working in the garden all summer. She sighs and is silent for a while.*

At last she raises her candid eyes to mine. How I long for the winter, *she admits,* when I can stay in the house all day treading wool shag that sprouts between my toes like grass. I shall pad about the sunroom trying this chair and that until I find one to my comfort and settle my bum into the cushions and hoist my feet up on the padded footstool. There I shall sit and watch them grow whiter by the day, sometimes even by the hour, at my side a pile of the largest and longest books I can find in the library. God grant that some of these will yield tales both pathetic and heroic, for only in such stories can I find that optimistic sadness which holds my attention and brings pride to my heart and new tears to my eyes.

I shall rise only to make coffee and sandwiches or to visit the bathroom—even this I shall do reluctantly. By March I shall hardly be able to move from my chair to my bed from my bed to my chair.

Then one day spring will appear again with its flurry of digging and seeding, and I shall forget that I ever said this or did it. Thus will my life wear on from season to season, from equinox to equinox until one spring I shall find myself unable to get up from my chair, my book, my melancholy. I shall be left gazing through the window at my daughter, herself by this time grown into a stout grandmother, or at least a great-aunt, walking barefoot between the rows of the garden, a measure of carrot seed held lightly in her palm. From time to time she will rest from her continual bending and flinging and stare up at the lead blue of the sky which threatens, or perhaps promises, rain.

The Usual Dream About One's Own Funeral

and here comes the worshipful company
driving up in dark and polished
cars, circa 1933,
rather rusted round the fenders
but still a good drive

there is my shorthair cousin
the one that works in a bank
aunts in knitted hats
my niece, my godchild
not seen since the christening
for lack of white she wears
a print of wild roses blurred
and faded by the salty air,
she sits in the highgrass
eating a sandwich
her long hair roughed
and snaggled by the wind

a pity someone forgot
I should have been sewn up
shipshape in a sail   the coffin
is green though, carapace
and plastron bossed as a turtle shell

mud to mud intones the pastor
his good boots sinking
into the shore ooze
flowers are the stunted silverweeds
with square blossoms
the colour of goldfish

and oh in my girlhood
those burials at sea
a signal of dark flags
hung down between the masts
pipescreech at the sinking of the corpse
*   and those memorials*
*   for drowned sailors*
when the band played
and wreaths, some of them
with lighted candles, floated
out on the swell
towards blue water

they never returned
but sometimes after a storm
I would find metal clips and hoops
beached and tangled

salt crust on the slough's lip
licked from the teeth
tasted in a strong westerly
looking out on a sea of dry grasses
bent all one way

while the pale girl
combs her snarled hair
with a comb white as fishbone
dipped in the brackish
curl of water

seas diminish, diminish
and die, as she laces
a green ribbon
through the knotted swatch of her hair

A chocolate egg is made by binding two equal halves together.

When it is whole, balance it on the pointed end and spin. Eventually it will waver and fall on its side (but which side?) and roll. Never again will you be able to tell which half was right, and which was left.

Or indeed whether the egg is divided N/S or E/W.

But it's true, isn't it, that before something has become a whole we may not refer to it as divided? The trick of a word, the sag of the language, may mean it has always been whole, even before the two halves were joined. Apartness. Agglutination.

Invent me a set of pure symbols. Write me a letter in unmistakeable signs. But are these signs unmistakeable from each other, or are they simply unmistakeably signs?

Now give me an imaginary number; speak me an imagined word.

Resurrection. The tomb opened. An egg broken cleanly, perfectly apart.

over and over a woman is told that she's not what she seems to be   at first she fights this *I am* she says *what I seem to be:*   sand, twigs, stones, and waves of disturbed air through which a bird has just flown, also light refracted from the lid of a syrup tin the disc of light wobbles on the floor and ceiling

she begins to have second thoughts   perhaps after all she is not what she seems: a laurel hedge, a butterfly flagging on the beach, a scale from the wing of that butterfly, a rhubarb bush, the oiled wheel of a train

she could indeed be something not yet mentioned not yet named for always she tells herself *before you have finished naming a thing the meaning has changed* no one can speak as fast as a thought darts across the mind   no one can speak faster than the sound of words

I'm not what I seem to be she confesses at last then a warm subservience floods through her and she becomes the fluent shadow of any names we may choose to throw at her

One morning in late spring a young woman wakens alone on a strange shore. When she sits up and looks about her she sees that she has been sleeping in the sheltered hollow between two sandhills. All around her the low dunes are spread with patches of seaholly and spike grass. Because it is not yet summer the grass is still sharply green and the holly's glaucous leaves are still pliant in their papery bracts.

She gets to her feet and looks eastward. At first all she can see is endless quilted sand, but when she shades her eyes and looks into the sun she can just make out a narrow strip of ocean glittering in the brilliant light. It is as though the sea were a snail which has felt the land's thrust as the prod of a finger, and has shrunk back immediately into its shell of pearly sky and distance.

The woman has no idea where she has come from. All she knows is that the journey took many days, weeks perhaps, even a month. She has travelled from a great city in another country but has forgotten the name of that place, the names of her companions, even her own name. She is ragged and travel-weary, but happier than she has ever dreamt of being.

My hands are fishes
Loosed from the angler's barb,

she sings clearly in a language she has never heard before,

My feet are otters
Sprung from the trap.

Sometime later, she tells herself, she may bring to mind that other place, those other people, that other language. But for now she is content to wander on the beach foraging for food and naming everything she sees in the new words which come so freely to her tongue.

A Celebration

Our grandmother had gout
(I think it was that)
there were chalk deposits on her knuckles
that stuck right through the skin
she used to amuse us children
by drawing five simultaneous lines
on the blackboard with the back of her hand
it must have been painful

last summer she died

she was drowned in the sea on her birthday
while swimming off Portland Head
it was a cool and windy day
but nothing would keep her
from the stormy water

they buried her on the southdowns
under a hummock of grass

But those limey spikes
grew rapidly in that soil
they branched underground
like the twigs of a great tree
they grew upwards from her desiccating hands

by September they poked out at the surface
a wide circle of little chalky stubs
I think they might have leafed out amongst the short grass but
autumn is a poor time for sprouting

when All Souls' came we lighted
eighty of them for holy candles
they burned brightly for a while
and then they wrinkled and browned
and flickered out

next year they may flower with rockroses
or stiff honeycomb corals

that's one of the reasons
we are waiting and hoping for the spring

A Thistle
CALLED
HOLY

On The Sun

Journeys are all circular.
There's someone at the centre holding

The swung pail from which no water falls.
There's someone holding

The lunging rope, someone blindfold
In the middle of the game.

So round and round
Round and round you go,

The whole earth round.

O pony on the beaten lunging track
Do you imagine you're making a new claim

To earth's old journey?

Ah, Sun-flower weary of time,
Who counth the steps of the sun;
Seeking after that sweet golden clime,
Where the traveller's journey is done. (WM BLAKE)

You are the one who moves on his axis,
Turning that cheek, this cheek
To the warmth of the sun.

Round and round on the twisted neck
Of a green stem
The corolla with its ray florets

Swinging to the lights of sunrise
Of sunset.

Never deceive such a flower,
Advises the old herbalist

With lanterns or torches for in five days
It will twist its head off.

It's the backend of the year. Purple loosestrife wands stand black and dry in the garden. We can hear their papery scratching above the traffic, below the gusting wind.

The chaffy seeds fall as we watch. Who could believe the urgency of that scattering? More than a poet desires fame, or a traveller his bed, each one of these seeds desires its own resurrection. But why should God, who after all did not heed the desperate prayer of his only Son, spare even a moment's thought for a loosestrife seed?

Nevertheless the seeds do not give up. With their innocence, with their patience they beseech Him night and day. They think of their rustling as a voice repeating over and over, "Be ashamed, O God, be ashamed of your dryness, your lack of words. How is it that the very wind speaks, but you do not answer us?"

After several weeks of drought, their Lord at last allows the rain of His mercy to fall down upon them. Most of the seeds drown in this sudden outpouring of love, but a few simply float it out and are saved. After the flood abates, these manage to take root in another part of the garden. But things are not all that good. The soil is soggy and cold, and fine white worms crawl up from the mud and feed on the delicate new leaves. The seedlings feel they have enough evidence to lodge a formal complaint.

God sends a mediator, an angel with double qualifications, she is both a botanist and an ecologist, to deal with their foolish arrogance. Come, come, she says, you must agree that we can't allow the whole garden, let alone the whole planet, to find itself twenty inches deep in purple loosestrife.

Well how did she figure that one out? Can she, a mere angel after all, have come to understand the relationships of all created things? Of course not. Like the rest of us, she has just enough knowledge to deal with the question in hand.

As always, the long winter allows us to forget the existence of purple loosestrife until March, when you and I find ourselves sitting knee to knee before the hearth, leafing through the garden catalogues.

To our surprise, no mention is made of seeds. However, there are vivid descriptions of many flowering perennials, including loosestrife, in several shades of pink and purple. Instructions for planting the carefully divided roots are given in great detail. On the back cover of every catalogue is a nicely designed order form with the cheerful slogan: GOOD LUCK WESTERN GARDENERS IN THE COMING SEASON.

you speak in a dry voice of the sunburnt skin on the face of the woman who tells through a mouthful of grit of an unpainted house scoured by the sun where she stands on an old chair with a thin rag in her hand trying to clean the window where dirt has lodged in the corners of the frame

she tells of when you were a boy lying face up in a field of many-coloured clover set upon by bees their humm humm bumble-bees groundbees purring in their furry bodies you see them huge as cats leaping from the clover flowers and chasing you down the gravel road through a wire fence and into a field of tall green wheat where you crouch breathless with your hands around the back of your neck trying to ward off those darts from piercing the delicate flesh behind your earlobes

the hum grows louder and louder it comes from overhead where one lazy plane is flying and now the earth tilts so that the sky is below you are falling into a pit of sky deeper than the slough deeper than the well

slowly through space you fall more than a month you name the days as you fall you write the names with a white pencil of smoke on the walls of the sky

on the fourth sunday you see that at last you are approaching the plane a silver insect not at all like a bee it is tin like a christ-mas present its edges sharp as a toy car hood

after dinner you play in the yard with your new toy you don't need winter boots because there is no snow *this is a black christ-mas* your mother explains *it is dark all over there is a war on we must pray for peace and* she ties her new red kerchief very tight under her chin outside it is stony cold the pebbles under your feet are sharp you can see the pointed stars they sting your eyes with their light the yard is silvery not black you throw the tin plane up it falls into the trough where a foal is drinking there is ice on the foal's lip

humm humm humm the airplane flies through the night the passengers are singing as they fly *you are younger than you were in the summer* they sing *you are getting younger all the time soon you will shrink down to a baby small enough to get back into your mother you will ride inside her all winter you will hear the squelch of the floormop you will hear the squeak of the cloth as you try to clean the corners of the window*

while you were away while you were off in the sky the woman and the house have crumbled and blown away now there is just one wall left standing just one window with no glass through it you can see the prairie and far away the crumpled riverbed under the window stands an old chair with a rung missing and a stained cooking pot full of rain where a bumblebee is collecting water for her family, they live in a hole in the ground

and dryly you explain to your child how the sun is really an image of our idea of the sun just as the prairie is a reflection of our need for flatness *consider* you tell him *the clever dance of the bee which is in the exact shape of her idea of distance*

the window opens onto a garden where it is early summer beyond the garden are two hayfields newly mown and beyond the hay an ocean lying painfully white in the sun

it is washday and specks of suds light as spittlebug froth float aimlessly into the room where someone not clearly seen is wiping them from the piano keys which trill dolorously under the stumble of heavy fingers sheathed in cotton dusting gloves the one moving slowly in the dim room is thought to be a woman because she is dusting because she shrinks from a stray bee which clings to the wallpaper trying to suck nectar from a printed rose

at dusk this same servant comes to close the casement against the bats which threaten to swoop in and tangle their thin claws in the upswept coiffes of the female heads, quite ten of them, which can be seen floating in the broad strip of lamplight reflected in the windowpanes

the servant watches the heads circle slowly opening their mouths as though to speak   but they think better of it and decide instead to nod distantly to one another while touching their cheeks to the polished edges of the mantelpiece and nuzzling the coarse linen pleats of the curtains

they are seeking for new places to hide during the long gloomy day when it always seems to them that the evening and the lamplight will never come *opening a door* nurse remarks to us children gathered around her knee *is much the same as answering a question*   it's true that some questions are never answered but that should not prevent us from asking them

and some little ones leave too soon for any questions to be asked let alone answered she adds regretting we know the tiny sister whose wax image we have lately buried in a small white box decorated with all the wildflowers of late august   *she has gone before* nurse explained at the time gently tidying the careless mounds of nosegays and wreaths

but we know better   we know that the real baby is hidden somewhere around the house for when we awake in the night we often hear thin wailing cries and nurse's voice shushing the child she has put away for the winter   *you'll see* mary reassures us   the very first warm day in march she'll fetch out baby beryl and plop her into the high pram for an airing along the gravel walks of mr cardoman's garden

the garden of course is not really mr cardoman's it used to belong to grandmother and now it belongs to mother and perhaps even a little to father however none of us is about to give the gardener this terrible news *not after all the work he does day in and day out* and lucretia soberly presses her lips together managing to sound and look very like nurse in one of her proper moods

it is almost november and mr cardoman is getting things shaped up for the winter   shan't be any mould on *his* grass come spring   as soon as the leaves are raked and taken away he sets about the shrub roses with his secateurs and his pruning knife *you young'uns don't stand there* gormless he snaps *pick up them twigs and bits and pile 'em in the wheelbarrer look sharp now*   in spite of the thorns we all three set to work at once feeling more honoured than we can say for the old man hardly ever says a word to us let alone asking for our help

when all the leaves and twigs are gathered he takes a shovel with a pointed end and begins to mound the roots of the roses with dirt against the coming frost   that's when we spy the key sticking out of the earth   *pounced on it like three robins on a worm* the gardener laughs nastily but he doesn't take the key away prudent mary dusts it off and puts it in the pocket of her pinafore

there it stays for quite a while lucretia and I wondering has she forgotten it? will it go to the laundry and get mangled in mrs purdy's mangle?

but mary has simply polished it clean and put it away in the velvet-lined drawer of her private writing box   one day after christmas when it's snowy and blowy she brings it out and hands it round for us to admire   *now we can begin opening things* she declares and there's never a doubt that the key will fit them all desks and closets and chests and the door of a secret room at the top of the house the possibility of which is just now forming at the back of our minds

SIÔN FOREST

look you are this
and this one, a man
with a fine but crooked nose
a woman who wryly says
of her breasts that they are
like those lidded enamel jugs
left at farm gates for
milking-girls to fill
out of kindness
each can with its painted name
Granny Gruffudd, Old Tewdr,
Phylip the Mail, who had
it shot off in the war
and was rewarded
with the perpetual job
of postmaster

and aren't you that man
who got new teeth and cried
with the pain of them
all night and every
night for a week, his wife
rubbing his gums with balsam
weed and bringing him dillwater
in the baby's christening cup?

yes you are that and that one,
Mrs Salisbury, Mrs Jones
come to glean little potatoes
in our hill fields
and Huw from up the mountain
who kills the pigs

and you are the one, Siôn Forest
lying beside me in the night
after the hay's cut and I
awaken in the first hour
of the new day listening
in the storm to the rain
pour down on the mown timothy
and fescue

I can smell dark mildew
already rotting the hay
whose seeds fall damp
and useless to the ground
I count them and they are
as many as you are Siôn
sleeping and waking

FLATBREAD

I have a great mind or I had a great mind once
I used to walk about in a coastal city

or my body when upright
makes an L with the prairie

now I live in a fieldstone hut
some of it has tumbled down
and I believe
in the aesthetic of simplicity

this is my pancake
baked on a hot stone
I have ground the grain myself
it is wild grain
from the shallows of a lake

I fold the pancake over and over and then across
I hold it in the curled palm of my hand
I place it in the empty curve of my mouth
it tastes sweet and gritty
I am satisfied

with my blanket and rock pillow
I prepare for the night

lying in the flat darkness
I dream the corruption of mountains
the splitting of slatey ledges
the crumbling of peaks

The child writes his name in wet sand with a bent stick. The edges of the letters are rough, but the intention is clearer than the sky.

The woman is leaping among the waves. Seasprite, she tells herself, or something like it. She's admiring her knees as they bend and straighten, admiring her belly as it emerges wet and firm from the foam, her hands as they open and close like anemones.

She's imagining that she remembers the time when scaly creatures emerged from the ocean. She thinks of the giving up of scales for smooth skin, the return to scales, the exchanging of these for fur, the time of feathers—now where does that fit in?

Such questions don't trouble the child. Not enough lifetime has passed for him to forget where he came from. He's not about to look back. His desire is to remain always on shore, stepping on the earth, making himself known to the land.

The man wades into the water after something he has glimpsed among the algae and the sealilies. He dips his hand in deep and brings up a beautiful thing, a thighbone. He shouts the triumph of discovery, of finding a treasure.

The man, the woman, and the child are standing around this rod of yellowed matt ivory. No, says the woman, it is more brownish than yellow. It is the colour of a mulatto's skin. And she picks up the bone and kisses it; you might think it was flesh, lips not bone. Her eyes are closed when she does it.

The man understands that this belonged to a young fellow, a cabin boy perhaps on his first voyage, one who had not yet experienced the disappointment of lost desire. Look how strong it is. Look how smooth. Look how graceful its shape. Tears burn the back of his eyes.

The child laughs and throws away his stick. He picks up the bone and carries it across the sand to a dry firm patch. With it he writes his name. The edges of the letters are as smooth as a calm sea.

OUR FIRST GODS WERE FISHES

Our first gods were fishes,
for how could we not worship
the elegance of their ribs
the economy of their entrails?

Each spring we watched the passion
of their spawning, saw how their fingerlings
swarmed in the light of the green shallows.

Our lines were twisted hair,
our hooks barbed thorns.

Crouched in the fire's circle
we passed flakes of delicate flesh
from hands to crossed hands, then at a signal
all at once we swallowed our holy ones,
and our bodies became theirs. Our dance
the sudden twist and dash of emerald minnows.

Lately these gods, these fishes
turn up in the interior of split rocks.
Fleshless their bones' white combs.
Valiantly they swim against a current of stone,
opening their mouths to swallow the drought of rock
as though it were the sea.

Now, far from any body
of water sweet or bitter,
we live between the cliffs of the city,
brick walls so high
there's no way of knowing
whether there is anything beyond this
netted trap, this compound
sentence.

Nothing for it but to look upward
to our hope far past the pigeons
burbling on their ledges,
higher even than the falcon's gyre.

And there they are, flying fishes
playfully leaping the blue waves
of upper air, then suddenly regrouping,

Their sober schools
crossing with certainty
the white straits of the clouds.

THE ELEPHANT DREAM

the elephant dream is for spring
when we paint the outside of the house
you go downtown to buy a ladder
but instead you purchase
a rather old sway-backed elephant

the elephant stands quietly under the dormer windows
you stand on its broad back
carefully painting the window frames
a gallon of white paint
is balanced on the animal's head

when it is my turn to paint,
the elephant, in spite of its size,
objects to my sturdy weight
it lopes away across the prairie
with me clinging to its ears
it rears and screams horribly
white paint pours down one side of its trunk

you bravely give chase
and skilfully capture the beast
lock it in the small back porch of our house

the elephant breaks the windows
scattering glass into the flowerbeds
then, after a whole minute of silence
we hear the terrible pouring
it is pissing out its huge elephant bladder
the floor is knee-deep in urine
we can hear the elephant sloshing about inside
trumpeting its triumph

meanwhile we stand about in the yard
watching ragged puffs of honey-smelling steam
escape through the broken panes

THE BURNING MAN

First interpretation: He's escaping from a flaming cottage with his beard on fire. The three women he's left in there to burn are his mother, his wife, and his daughter. Some say he set the fire himself, having made up his mind to a fresh start in life with his neighbour, a buxom seamstress.

Another explanation: He's a lifelong student of the law. One day he's walking through the forest and smells smoke, comes upon a cabin in flames. He considers. Shouldn't he at least make an attempt to save the three sisters who live there? He takes out his watch and sees that ten minutes have passed during this cogitation. He realizes that now he has time to rescue only one. That's his dilemma. Which one shall he save? Better be fair about it and let them all burn. He is, after all, a serious man. In some dark perfect way he believes in justice above all.

Yet appearances are important to a man of his standing, and he takes out his cigarette lighter and sets his beard on fire, but not before he has made sure that the fire truck is approaching. He's certain that the firemen will have no trouble putting out his small personal conflagration.

Third interpretation The fellow is an alchemist who has lived for many years in the depths of the woods. During all that time he has worked to conjure gold.

This morning he has at last succeeded. But inadvertently his efforts have caused his retort to blow up, releasing the dread female spirits of silver, antimony and copper into the material world. Their anger at thus being rudely transported shows itself in the vindictive way they have set fire to his fine beard. In the end his gold is consumed in the flames and he's lucky to escape with his nose.

Now these are just three stories, and surely there must be plenty more explanations for a man's beard to burst into flames. As a matter of fact, I've heard of an itinerant storyteller who has made his fortune extrapolating from just this one image. In all his wanderings, or so they say, he has never told the same tale twice.

More than that, I know the very woman who day after day sits by the river's edge dipping her knuckly fingers first into the shining water and then into all the colours of the mind. She is the one, she claims, who has created every image that has ever had its face turned up on the table of divinations.

Never mind that as I watch her spread out her hands, I can always see grey rivermud under her nails. Streaked grey, the colour of an aging man's beard.

Here in the saintly dark, all is so cleanly dank, all is ordered and cradled. Nothing is sinful. Even the suck of the worm's mouth upon us is preordained, therefore right.

Suddenly, it's dawn up there. It comes with the silver squeal of birds, a sound like thin trumpets. "Crack the box," it says. "Arise, this is the day."

Obedient as buds, our heads appear in the open grass, and a rain of golden yods falls down upon us. So this is light. We had forgotten it.

We, who lay long in holy depths of earth, have all at once become small and new, can't even remember our names, and the passers-by won't tell us. They stop. They smile. They stare and then move on.

At last a child in blue cotton leans down to us. "Daffs," she says, and, taking each of us by the neck, yanks for the love of God.

What Is A Man To Do

What is a man to do when the tree he loves is rotting at its
centre?

What is a woman to do when the man she loves is pale as a
sickly tree?

He's leaning over, he's falling slowly, like the curled crest
of a wave of the sea. Like the tide

going out. It's the salt kills the tree, says the old man, the
salt that preserves the wood

My cheeks are burning, he says, there's a pain like a
swordfish in my side.

Two women are walking the yellow old man
up and down the beach,

to give him a bit of sea air, they say, nodding wisely,
looking into each others' eyes.

They stumble him along the dirty strip of sand to the edge of the
tide where he can find water to dabble his crusty old
toes.

Look there, says he to his wife and grownup daughter, there's
a deadhead bobbing out there

like an old man taking to the ocean
kicking at crabs and flotsam
swallowing fishes and boats on his way out

like a faithless lover hurrying to a new liaison foolishly
hoping to root in the dirt
of another, a distant shore.

My father was born in a distant country where every person is a tree—every adult that is.

Children are fieldflowers, they are grass, they are lilies and poppies and small blue lupines. Until puberty, they are any plants they choose. More than that, they may change their minds as many times as they wish. A child may wake as a gillyflower and go to sleep as eglantine. Is it any wonder that, in that country, no one is in a hurry to grow up?

At the age of twelve or so, each must name a tree and is stuck with this choice until the tree falls from age, or is struck down by the axe of the woodcutter. This last is their way of explaining the death of the young in battle, for, in spite of their worship of the peaceable plant, they are a warlike lot.

All this my father told me, but though I bothered and cajoled him, he would never say which tree he had chosen or whether, in this new country, he still felt bound by the customs of his birthplace.

He always seemed just a man to me, and very like other people's fathers: that is, strong and infallible in my childhood and, as I advanced into adolescence, more and more clumsy and overbearing.

There was one difference though. Unlike other men he was never seen without a shirt or a sweater. Not that he was particularly modest in other ways. Several times I caught him pulling on his trousers in a hurry. I had a good look. Nothing strange there. But what was he hiding beneath his T-shirts and button up cardigans? Was he afraid of woodpeckers? Was there a hole there, beneath his heart, where a squirrel had made her nest?

I was almost a grown woman when he took me for a holiday in a warmer part of the country. It was May and already early summer in that gentle climate. He pointed out a tree I had never seen on the Prairies and acknowledged it as his own. *Hippocastanum* he explained proudly. Its leaves were huge green hands, and between them sprung tall racemes of bloom like white and yellow candles. This then was my father's tree, generous in its spread, amazing in its summer complacency.

We stood there, hand in hand, as he told me about its various phases, of how in fall it would bear inedible brown nuts in leathery green cases, nuts that are the weapons of little boys in their battles.

All this was years ago, and my father is dead now, hollowed and fallen like every tree before him. I was with him when he died.

No sooner had he taken his last breath than I leaned over him and began to unbutton his pyjama jacket. What did I expect to find? Simply the chest of an old tired man, the tangles of coarse grey hair intricate as twigs, the nipples hard and resinous as winter buds.

MALUS

I look out the window at a seedling crab which has volunteered in the middle of my windflower patch. How to explain my sudden love for this small but uppity thing?

I'm resolved to watch day by day to make certain that it has everything it needs, rain and grief, sunlight and resignation. I couldn't love it more if I had planted it myself.

When you live in a house like mine where every door opens upon an angel standing on his haloed head and his nightie stiff around his legs, a tower of starched muslin, where every pot on the shelf is home to a tiny priest as small as a spider, his stole about his shoulders ready to hear confession, then you'll know that happiness is the contemplation of outdoor growing things their natural order keyed and adamant.

My darling seedling will you flourish? When you're a sapling will you remember who watered you on dry days? And will I still love you when you're four times my height, your boughs full of blossoms and birdsnests? The blossoms fall and the eggs hatch, such a cheeping and squawking to be fed. Thank God when all are fledged and flying. I was almost ready to pay a woodsman to lop everything to the nub.

Leaves obscure the sky as I pray for bitter apples luminous with knowledge, and, when these are fallen, for enough wasps to feed in the splits and brown bruises, enough buzz to drown out the whirr of the holy man's wheel as he chants cross-legged on the grass under the yellowing leaves, while beside him, its dignity not wavering, sits a black dog lustrous and silent as a monk.

A Thistle Called Holy

for Tessa

she's writing her memoirs and wants to be left *alone alone alone*
she complains to her niece who has arrived dusty and tired from
riding a thousand miles across the plains on her motorcycle to
tell her how much she is admired in toronto

you are an inspiration the young woman stands by her bike and
reads from a prepared script *for you were not afraid to abandon
everything for your own innerness*

in the garden the aunt has planted adonis which raises its poi-
sonous pheasant eyes to heaven claiming to have sprung from
the blood of the god she has seeded calendula whose orange rays
signify the fleecy tresses of the magdalen *there is also a thistle
called holy* she murmurs quoting from the herbal

even the urban niece knows that thistles are eaten by donkeys
that later shit them out on the verges of narrow mountain roads
then comes auntie with her little shovel to gather the precious
buns which will nourish all kinds of herbs and fungi for dyeing
the yarn which she weaves back and forth while telling about
this and that incident from her past *ah the tapestry of life* she
sighs as she throws the shuttle

her niece is heartsick how can the old lady go on like this she
wonders when I believed in her and came all this way to greet
her in the name of my contemporaries   must everything end
here in this pampered garden with her botched weaving and her
trite words

Industrial Park—Midsummer

Bruno and I lay prone in the grass,
by turns boy and girl, by turns two brothers.

The year warmed our backs like sun on a lake.
The grass hid our shoulders but our bums stuck out;

some of our mothers' careful patches showed over the
long stalks just beginning to flower,

their panicles not yet ready to cast pollen on the
cheeks of our shorts.

The bottle of tepid water we passed between us was
glass green as stem juice.

We were watching five women build a tower of used
scaffolding. When they cut the dried-out wood, dust
rose like plumes of steam.

As they clambered up and down their rickety ladder
everything swayed, and yet the tower grew.

A child staggered over to them carrying a heavy tin of
old paint found somewhere in the broken and dead factory
behind us.

Starting at the top the women painted the slats a dull
black, the colour of dogpen fences.

And the tower was as tall as the two sad trees planted
here years ago.

Evening came, and the women were calling us to help
them. They handed us scissors and baskets.

Midnight came, and we had picked every flower from
every garden. We two cut all the pinks and mignonette.
Roses and lilies we left to the others.

By moonlight the women climbed up and down and covered
their tower from top to bottom with stolen flowers.

We began to sing, but they said wait until morning when
the sun comes up and the dew falls.

Word got around, and by eight a crowd had gathered.
Some swore and some cursed and an old man spat on the
child's face,

but she simply took a daisy and wiped away the spittle.
This was not a time for reprisals.

When the soldiers came it changed everything. We all
made a circle round the tower and began to dance and
sing.

Round and around we pranced, for all at once
we understood the meaning of this day, and that there
never would be another like it.

The soldiers got into their truck and left. Even here,
even now, you don't shoot people for picking flowers.

It was noon, and we two lying side by side eating the
day's bread, watching the Earth's blossoms wilt and
fall from the tower.

During last night the grass had grown tall enough to
hide us, ripe enough to dust us grey and yellow.

Our mothers called and they came looking, but they couldn't find where we hid listening to the crash and squeal of a shunting train.

And we knew then we had lain in the grass too long, and that whenever we got up to leave it would be too soon.

On the NATURE & HISTORY of ANGELS

An angel is not like a tangle of worms, but is very like the movement of a tangle of worms. A writhing like music in the bowels.

Music is the sound of flight, of these wingless ones beating the air with their truth and wisdom.

Ah, these messengers, wherever they go on the business of their God they carry a flame between them. That's why they fly in pairs, lest the winds of logic should blow out the light of faith.

The song of conclusion, the end of the universe is what every angel desires, or would desire if desire was part of the angelic nature.

It matters not to them that their Lord shows them neither favour nor love, that he casts them out upon the ether and reels them in on the taut line of his whim, for obedience, not love, is their creed.

It is said that angels having no souls cannot sin in the usual sense of the word, but if they were capable of wickedness then disobedience would be their undoing.

When Lucifer was kicked out of heaven all the lights went out. Spent matches, snuffed candles littered the floor of heaven. The only bright thing in the universe was the fire below, its glow showing the way home to all creation. This was not too bad for the fallen angels, but was hell for God and his holy ones.

Look up, crane your necks, it's August and the stars are falling. Does this mean there are angels still being cast out to wither in eternal space? God would have to be a fool to try it again.

As a precaution He has taken anger from them. In its place they were given spite and a yen for revenge. From an angel's point of view this has been an advantage.

The question is, have the angels ideas of their own? The answer is that the speculations of an angel, short, white and continually in motion are like threadworms infesting the system of a child.

What colour then is the inner being of a shining angel? What colour is the message that such a being brings the person visited?

Blue spirit, purple message, green presence.

We all know that angels have their own Bible. We learned in Sunday School that they, like the rest of us children, are supposed to read a chapter every night and commit six verses to memory. But what is memory to a being who is co-eternal with the universe?

One day long past, or one day soon, God opens his hand and there on his enormous palm lies that elegant codex, the Bible of the Angels. Not at all like our Holy Books which we have been forced through the ages to write ourselves, tears falling and sweat rising. Haven't we the ink-stained fingers to prove it?

How surprising then that contents of these writings is so much like those of our own Books. How familiar to us are these tales of conflict and revenge, these lists of wailings and recriminations.

There is, of course, no New Testament for angels. And if there were they'd refuse to read it. They claim that since they can tumble headlong, but not into sin, they have no need of redemption. If they fall they fall and cannot be forgiven to nestle joyfully in the bosom of the Eternal One.

Have you, like myself, always wanted to peek over an angel shoulder and read what is written in that Book with the sky blue cover? What can be the script on those pages? There are said to be ninety-nine earthly scripts but there must surely be a heavenly one. Oh, when shall we be allowed to read that hundredth script written in breath and fire?

Angels are fond of dancing and have a larger repertoire than all the ballet companies on Earth put together. Look how they bound and leap in the ozone layer, even in the atmosphere, how they frolic and twist and turn. Feathery and weightless as they are, their toes never bleed into pink satin shoes and there's not that clicking noise above the music. Instead they swirl like clouds, fountains of light, auroras.

ॐ ॐ ॐ

Angels, we tell ourselves, have dwelt in strange places. Either they do still or we have made up those tales:

The story of the angel who lived always up the nose of a certain pope. Sneeze as he might he could never get rid of that holy presence. He was never free of the spirit of chastity and sacred compliance. What a difficult thing that must have been for a pope. It's impossible not to feel sorry for him.

The story of the angel who inhabits the left eye of that glossy black dog—that metaphor of power and seduction, that animal that sits in the back of the car breathing down the neck of the mother as she conducts the vehicle of life, bravely driving on through white blizzards and dark rainstorms. Stopped at the traffic lights she turns around for just one glimpse of his red eyes glowing yet cold. That's when the angel leaps to the woman's chilly fingers taking over the steering, taking over the power, taking away her reason for being, her usefulness in this world.

Never mind about that dog, what about cats? Can any creatures who were once worshipped as minor deities, who were once mummified in hopes of the resurrection, see themselves demoted to the state of beings a little lower than those who are a little lower than the angels? After all angels don't even have fur. Why should they get all the beautiful names—Gabriel, Azreal, Michael—while cats, who after all are of divine origin, have to put up with Kitty, or worse still Pussy. This is their message yowled to Heaven, but God never receives it. This is partly because the angels intercept it and muffle the sharp edges of their cat voices. But largely because these arrogant felines insist on addressing God as Bast. We all of us know that God's name begins with A or Y or J or E. The angels, of course, have heard the word Demiurge but are wise enough never to let it pass their seraphic lips.

One day a child goes into the sweetshop with a handful of copper coins. She chooses two sugar mice, one sugar angel. She eats the mice down to their string tails. Now for the angel. She bits off its head and swallows it. She licks away at the blue sugar wings. Her tongue is stained with cheap indelible dye. She wraps the rest in her handkerchief and throws it into the river. The hankie unfurls and sinks, but the angel floats on as though it had some kind of purpose. At last it leaps over the falls and is lost in the spume. Perhaps in the end it plunged upwards, riding headless into the ultimate sky.

"Oh, that I had wings of angels," sing the children in Sister Gertrude's choir, "here to spread and heavenward fly." But do angels have wings, other than those that we have imagined for them?...No, no they swim through space, ozone and atmosphere, just as jellyfish swim in the oceans. Their messages are precise and clear, but they themselves are amorphous creatures, sometimes opaque, sometimes translucent, armless, finless, not always faceless. Root about in any vacant lot and you'll find them, shards of amber beer bottles, scrunched-up gum wrappers, torn rubber safes, plastic-coated diapers. Wildflowers in the grass, birdshit on the water fountain.

Once long ago, when I was still her child, my mother told me that angels had beaten a path to her door. The house was called Stranger's Corner, and perhaps she thought of angels as the only strangers she could tolerate in her old garden with the leaning damson tree. I went out to look at the squashed grass, a new path between the perennial borders. Yes, it was trodden, but whether by children or goats I could not at first make out. Then Molly pointed to the footprints and they certainly didn't look human. "They each have only three toes." She explained, "If they are not birds then what's to stop them from being angels?"

AFTERWORD

On *Glassy Wings* includes selections from all my published collections—indeed all my poetry books except one. *Wild Man's Butte,* a long poem for voices aired on CBC and published by Coteau Books in 1979, is the exception. This work was written in collaboration with Terrence Heath, and the collaboration is so close that I cannot now distinguish which of the lines, or parts of lines, was written or first suggested by Terrence or by myself.

These poems were written from 1956 to 1997, though none of them was published in book form before 1974. This means that they span 41 years of my writing life. Looking through them, I realize that my attitude towards poetry has not changed much during these years. Indeed, it has hardly changed at all since I memorized and recited (I could not of course read or write at the time) my first childish efforts somewhere between my fourth and fifth birthdays. Later, at about the age of twelve, I decided that if the literary arts can be thought of as a mountain, then poetry is at the very peak. The pointy tops of mountains are no doubt the smallest part. The air is more rarified up here and there is snow under your boots, but then you are as near the heavens as you can get while still having your feet on the ground. Well worth the climb, wouldn't you say?

The abiding interests of a writer, indeed of any artist, must inform her art. My own interests include history, gardening, theatre, mycology, languages, botany, religions, and cooking, of course. Some, perhaps all, of these can be found in my work. Stronger than any mere interest though is my belief in transformation through metamorphosis. One thing or person or thought inevitably becomes another, and another, and another until it may at last return to the very form in which it first appeared. This I would say is not so much a set of relationships as it is a journey, not from here to there but from theophany to theophany.

A favourite thing to ask a poet is what are his or her literary influences. Well, what have been mine? There have been, over a long writing life, so many that it's not easy even to recall or list them. Shall I cite Baudelaire, ap Gwillym, Eliot, HD, van Eist? Then what of the Rosettis, Raine, Wordsworth, of Herrick and Thomas and Pound? Better that I confine myself here to the influence of the incomparable William Blake. A testy man perhaps, but a visionary poet who saw the world as it really is—"If the doors of perception were cleansed," he tells us, "then everything would appear to man as it is, infinite."

I could not have been more than four years old when my mother first read me Blake's *Songs of Innocence*, those enigmatic and unchildlike poems that tell of another time and place full of lambs and lost children. Thence to *Songs of Experience*, a place and time even more sinister and disturbing.

On then to the long poems with their extraordinary Bible-like rhythms and phrases, and to the *Memorable Fancies*. What have we here? Out with the moralistic, in with the prophetic, the visionary. Angels appear everywhere, and they are fierce and demanding rather than sweet and caring. And wasn't it Mr. B. who taught me that the body is an emanation of the spirit?

During my life I have found myself in various places— England, Wales, France, the Low Countries, and Germany are some of them. Each one of these has had an influence on my writing. Then there are the countries that I wish I had inhabited—Chile, East Africa, Finland, Lithuania. All I can do is hear their people singing or drumming in the distance: imaginary journeys to imaginary countries, imaginary mountains surrounding dreamed-of seas.

Is it really other places that have influenced my poems, or is it other languages? Some of these poems do indeed have titles in Welsh, Netherlandish, or Polish, some of the languages (and therefore places) that have come to my tongue at times during my writing life. What does this mean—simply that I hope to have entered these various thought-patterns and made them partly my own? Perhaps, but looking back I see that it is place that has influenced my work even more than language.

In 1951 when I found myself, quite against my will, on the Canadian Prairies—Saskatchewan, to be specific—I was homesick for Europe for only one year. My experience with Saskatoon and the rural southern part of the province convinced me that here was a land where poetry could be written, spoken, and sung for its own sake. It was not so much the land that influenced me, but this extraordinary sky, a sky which has no limits but those that the poetic mind cares to put on it. If I had stayed in Britain, or indeed any part of Europe, I would certainly have written poetry all my life, but it would have been much more cramped and circumscribed, more conventional and less absurd.

One experience sticks in my mind. We were living just north of the Big Muddy wilderness, not far from the United States border. The land was bare, rolling, boulder-strewn. The birds were mostly shore birds who seemed to be at home on the edges of the salt lakes and the brackish sloughs. There were no trees for songbirds to nest in, but there were colonies of bank swallows in the sandy cliffs round some of the lakes and there were horned larks nesting dangerously in the short dry grass. The plants were not at all the ones I had seen and collected in the environs of Saskatoon. Here things were tough and salty, therefore the wild plants were short and tough and often prickly as the cactus which grew all around. Snakes and coyotes and ground squirrels abounded. A wonderful country indeed.

It was here, when walking under a sky clear and blue as water, that I saw a small white cloud floating rapidly across the emptiness. It slowed down. And as I gazed at it a bolt of lightning came out of the cloud and hit the prairie. I could almost see the hand of Old Nobodaddy throwing down his fiery spear. I took this to be a command to get on writing my poetry, something I had neglected for the last few years, for though I heard it resonating in my head all the time I had not written it down. I started with a pencil and notebook. Then I bought a crotchety little typewriter from a neighbour who didn't know why he had wanted it in the first place. I was on my way, and my poems with me.

On Glassy Wings is a selection of all the poems I have written and spoken since then. There are memories of the places I lived in as a young person as well as pieces from my present life. These are journeys of place and time, from language to language. But is this all? Of course not.

Like any other poet's, my work is concerned with speculations and uncertainties, with dreams and insights, with metamorphoses and epiphanies. It is peopled with lovers and strangers, with animals and angels. It is set in gardens and deserts, in building lots and forests and farms, in places like a certain village "where time has come to an end."

—*Anne Szumigalski*

from WOMAN READING IN BATH *(1974)*
    Skeps in the Orchard
    Videotape
    Crabseeds
    Where are You Arthur Silverman?
    Ribgrass
    Nettles
    It Wasn't a Major Operation
    Ergot and After
    Long Distance
    Bertha
    Victim
    Early Sorrow
    Stopover
    Prospect House
    In the Wilderness
    What a Girl Has
    Woman Reading in Bath
    The Holy Fountain
    The Man from Toledo
    Granny Looks at the Stars
    A Celebration

from A GAME OF ANGELS *(1980)*
    A House With A Tower
    Grey-eyed Frances
    Daisy Filman
    Childermas   Three
    A Game of Angels
    Patrick Valentine
    The Name of Our City
    Sitting Under Death's Rich Shade
    About My War

Alice Long
The Usual Dream About One's Own Funeral
Siôn Forest
Flatbread
The Elephant Dream

from DOCTRINE OF SIGNATURES *(1983)*
Our Sullen Art
Fennec
Want of ♭ Want of Ð
The Musicologist
Hedera Helix—the Spiral
Evangelium
The Varying Hare
Honny
Heroines
Lavinia
Annwfn
Hanner Hwch Hanner Hob—the Flitch
Mates
Shrapnel
The Arrangement
Summer 1928
The Farm
In the Heat of the Morning
The Disc
The Bees
A Thistle Called Holy

from RISKS *(1983)*
extract

from INSTAR *(1985)*
Her Mother Being Dead in One Way or Another
The Cloud
Under the Glare of the Sun
Burning the Stubble

A Girl Dreams
The Restoration
The Margin
Dusk
The Undoing

from DOGSTONES *(1986)*
His Method
I Put On My Gloves
Mater Dolorosa
Desire
Looking for Uncle Tich in the War Cemetery
The Compassion

from JOURNEY/JOURNÉE *(1988)*
The Bear
On Parting
On Loneliness
On Singleness
An Offering
On Grieving
On the Sun

from RAPTURE OF THE DEEP *(1991)*
The Dove
The Cranes
Halinka
The Boy With His Head in His Hands at the
    Upstairs Window
As So Many Do
Viaticum—the Text
Gerald
Passover
Bigos
$i^2 = -1$
Purple
The Elect
The Fall

from VOICE *(1995)*

    Theirs is the Song
    Third Trimester
    Ferret
    Paradijslaan
    The Burning Man
    Malus
    Industrial Park—Midsummer

NEW POEMS

    Flick 1938
    Classification
    Your Child Looks Up
    In Praise of My Own Breasts
    Aunt's Story
    Making up a Four
    Wise Queenie, Wise Queen
    Green
    Between One Thing and Another
    Naked on the Shore
    Our First Gods Were Fishes
    What is a Man To Do
    On the Nature and History of Angels

SOME NOTES ON THE POEMS

INDUSTRIAL PARK—MIDSUMMER: This is an attempt to tell the story of the bands of peaceful protesters who travelled round the Polish countryside building towers of flowers during the Communist oppression.

PARADIJSLAAN *(Dutch):* The name of a narrow street in a working class district of Eindhoven, Holland

BIGOS *(Polish):* A famous hunter's stew.

ANNWFN *(Welsh):* The otherworld, perhaps more of a parallel world than an underworld. Often spelled *Annwn*.

HANNER HWCH HANNER HOB *(Welsh):* The title of a story from the Mabinogian which tells the tale of how pigs came to Wales.

A THISTLE CALLED HOLY *(Botanical): Carduus benidictus,* a plant much used in healing.

HIPPOCASTANUM *(Botanical): Aesculus hippocastanum,* the horse-chestnut tree.

MALUS *(Botanical): Pyrus malus,* the crab-apple tree.